What's the use of a house
if you haven't got
a tolerable planet to put it on?

. . .

NEW ENGLAND'S WHITE MOUNTAINS

At Home in the Wild

The finest workers in stone are not copper or steel tools,
but the gentle touches of air and water
working at their leisure
with a liberal allowance of time. . . .

Remember thy creator in the days of thy youth. . . .

Rise free from care before the dawn,
and seek adventures.

Let the noon find thee by other lakes,

and the night overtake thee everywhere at home.

. . .

There are no larger fields than these,
no worthier games than may here be played.
Grow wild according to thy nature, like these sedges and brakes,
which will never become English hay. . . .
Let not to get a living be thy trade, but thy sport.
Enjoy the land, but own it not.

—THOREAU

Whose woods these are I think I know
His house is in the village though;
He will not see me stopping here
To watch his woods fill up with snow.

My little horse must think it queer
To stop without a farmhouse near
Between the woods and frozen lake
The darkest evening of the year.

He gives his harness bells a shake
To ask if there is some mistake.
The only other sound's the sweep
Of easy wind and downy flake.

The woods are lovely, dark and deep.
But I have promises to keep,
And miles to go before I sleep,
And miles to go before I sleep.

—ROBERT FROST

NEW ENGLAND'S WHITE MOUNTAINS

At Home in the Wild

text by Brooks Atkinson and W. Kent Olson

photographs by Philip H. Evans, Amory B. Lovins,
and George DeWolfe

edited by Stephen Lyons

with a foreword by David R. Brower

APPALACHIAN MOUNTAIN CLUB / NEW YORK GRAPHIC SOCIETY · BOSTON

FRIENDS OF THE EARTH SAN FRANCISCO, LONDON, PARIS

We are grateful to the original publishers of the following works from which we have quoted herein:

Adams, John Coleman. "The Brook Path to Chocorua." Boston: *Appalachia*, AMC, 1893.

Atkinson, Brooks. *Skyline Promenades: A Potpourri*. New York: Alfred A. Knopf, 1925.

Bryant, William Cullen. "A Winter Piece," *The Poems of William Cullen Bryant, Selected and Edited, with a Commentary*, by Louis Untermeyer. New York: The Limited Editions Club, 1947.

Crawford, Lucy. *The History of the White Mountains*. Portland, Maine: B. Thurston & Co., 1846; or see *Lucy Crawford's History of the White Mountains, with an Introduction by Stearns Morse*, Hanover, New Hampshire: Dartmouth Publications, 1966.

Dillard, Annie. *Pilgrim at Tinker Creek*. New York: Harper's Magazine Press, 1974.

Frost, Robert. *Collected Poems*. New York: Holt, Rinehart, and Winston, 1963.

Hale, Nathan. *Notes Made During an Excursion to the Highlands of New Hampshire and Lake Winnipiseogee*. Andover, Mass.: Flagg, Gould, and Newman, 1833.

Josselyn, John. *An Account of Two Voyages to New England Made During 1638 and 1663*. Boston: W. Beazie, 1865.

Kugy, Julius. *Alpine Pilgrimage*. London: J. Murray, 1934.

Leopold, Aldo. *A Sand County Almanac, with Essays in Conservation from Round River*. New York: Oxford University Press, 1966.

Musgrove, Eugene R. *The White Hills in Poetry: An Anthology*. Boston: Houghton-Mifflin Co., 1912.

Spaulding, John. *Historical Relics of the White Mountains*. Washington, N.H.: J. R. Hitchcock, 1855.

Thoreau, Henry David. *Walden; Or, Life in the Woods*. Boston: 1854. *The Maine Woods*. Boston: 1864.

Ward, Julius. *The White Mountains: Guide to Their Interpretation*. New York: D. Appleton & Co., 1890. See also Anderson and Morse, *The Book of the White Mountains, 1930*.

Weygandt, Cornelius. *The White Hills*. New York: Holt & Co., 1934.

The lithographs are from William Oakes's *White Mountain Scenery* (Somersworth, N.H.: New Hampshire Publishing Co.) and Samuel Drake's *The Heart of the White Mountains: Their Legend and Scenery* (London: Chatto & Windus, Piccadilly, 1882).

We also thank *Yankee Magazine*, which published an earlier version of W. Kent Olson's "Lightning," and appreciate permission to quote from C. Francis Belcher's Encyclopedia of the AMC, which he carries in his head. We carry E. B. White's paragraph from *Stuart Little* in ours. The quotation from Frederick Law Olmsted *père* comes from a long lost paper written in 1865 and first published in 1952 in *Landscape Architecture* (Louisville, Kentucky: American Society of Landscape Architects).

New York Graphic Society books are published by Little, Brown and Company.
Published simultaneously in Canada by Little, Brown and Company (Canada) Limited

Published in San Francisco by Friends of the Earth, Inc., and simultaneously in Paris by Les Amis de la Terre and in London by Friends of the Earth Ltd.
ISBN: 0-913890-18-9
Lithographed and bound in Italy

Contents

Photographs

By Philip H. Evans (*PHE*), Amory B. Lovins (*ABL*), and George DeWolfe (*GD*).

The photographs in this book were taken over a seven-year period between 1971 and 1977. The cameras used ranged from 35 mm to 4 by 5, the lenses from 28 mm to 210 mm. The color shots were made with Kodachrome 25, the black-and-whites with Tri-X and Super-XX. Philip Evans acknowledges his gratitude for expert guiding by Dave Buchanan and equipment by Rich Wilcox, of Eastern Mountain Sports.

Foreword

NEW ENGLAND'S WHITE MOUNTAINS are the hills of home; they are lived in and shape the lives that live in them. Backyard mountains with backcountry in them, they are a little wildness close to home, to look at, to walk into, or simply to enjoy because it is there taking care of itself in its own delightful way. Stuart Little had a fair idea of what the White Mountains mean thanks to the good investigative reporting of E. B. White, who wrote about "the loveliest town of all, where the houses were white and high and the elm trees were green and higher than the houses, where the front yards were wide and pleasant and the back yards were bushy and worth finding out about, where the streets sloped down to the stream and the stream flowed quietly under the bridge, where the lawns ended in orchards and the orchards ended in fields and the fields ended in pastures and the pastures climbed the hill and disappeared over the top toward the wonderful wide sky. . . ." Towns can be lovelier still if the wide sky has White Mountains in it.

Less lovely towns are hard by. Two-thirds of the Americans who live in the United States live in the East, and about half of them live within a day's drive of the tiny wild backcountry of the White Mountain National Forest. It is to the eastern megalopolis what Central Park is to Manhattan. The ways lovers of the White Mountains use them could condemn this old range's backcountry to a slow death beneath encircling camps, ski courses cut through the forests, and millions of tramping or sliding feet.

The bearers of these feet can speak and vote; the bearers of forests cannot. Mountains can use a voice, and Frederick Law Olmsted was one of the first to try to speak for them. Recuperating in Yosemite from the strain of establishing Central Park, he proposed the rights for landscape implicit in the national park idea. The first requirement, he said, is to preserve the natural scenery and restrict within the narrowest limits the necessary accommodation of visitors. Structures should not detract from the dignity of the scene. "In permitting the sacrifice of anything that would be of the slightest value to future visitors," he wrote, "to the convenience, bad taste, playfulness, carelessness, or wanton destructiveness of present visitors, we probably yield in each case the interest of uncounted millions to the selfishness of a few."

Thus, in 1864, did an idea born on one coast reach another. Both coasts would contribute to its flowering. In 1868, just four years later, John Muir was in Oakland, having seen Central Park and fled west, telling the first person who asked where he wanted to go, "Anywhere that's wild." He found what he wanted in the Sierra—wildness, more than scenery, wild creatures that belonged there and domestic creatures that did not. Urged by an eastern editor to gather some friends together to save the Sierra from sheep, he founded the Sierra Club in 1892. The editor, Robert Underwood Johnson of *Century Magazine*, for which Muir had written, camped with Muir in Yosemite in 1889. Muir was persuasive; in 1890 Johnson had the bill introduced in Congress which established Yosemite National Park.

Perhaps Johnson suggested a mountain club because of what had happened in 1876 in Boston, when ninety-two men and eighteen women founded the Appalachian Mountain Club. The AMC had a once-known wilderness to restore. The Sierra Club had a little-known wilderness to rescue. Starting life a little bigger than the AMC (182 charter members to 110), it almost immediately plunged into vigorous legislative activity and has not let up.

At first both organizations gave most of their attention to the mountains they were born near. They grew slowly, the AMC comfortably in the lead. As the fifties began, the Sierra Club, nudged by The Wilderness Society, forty-three years its junior, decided to go national and to relearn what John Muir had taught it about the importance of wildness, extending its concern, as Muir had his, to the last great wilderness—Alaska's. The Sierra Club found itself contending with all the federal land agencies, getting deeper into legislative activity (and thereby losing its tax-deductible status), and carrying the battle for wilderness into the courts and overseas. It broadened its scope as it saw that cities and farms and commercial forests should be run better, and population be controlled, or the wilderness that civilization needed around it would be lost. The Sierra Club's rapid outreach did not arrive without inner conflict. One conflict led to the founding of Friends of the Earth in 1969. Muir's goals were now sought globally, and the combined membership of the Sierra Club and FOE grew to a quarter of a million. Like kindred organizations, with hundreds of millions of acres of wide-open spaces to be concerned about, they believed that they must persuade the federal government to spend the necessary money and the effort to manage and protect these places, with help now and then from the states.

In the White Mountains something quite else was happening, and the AMC was key to it. Antedating the Forest Service and the National Park Service—antedating even the Forest Reserve, most of the national parks, and the mapmaking functions of the Geological Survey—the AMC in its first quarter century concentrated on the exploration and mapping of the New England highlands, still uncharted. For two more quarter centuries the AMC strove to make the White Mountain region accessible through trails, a hut system, guidebooks, generous financial assistance, timely impatience, and well-placed influence. Senior to agencies and endowed with remarkable continuity, the AMC developed a kind of governance of its own. It could guide, interpret, oversee, and help house and rescue the throngs that visited one of the loveliest, and most heavily used, recreation areas of all.

Agencies may come and go. The AMC, we pray, is staying. Government bureaus should indeed go at the age of ten, Justice William O. Douglas once advised President Franklin D. Roosevelt, lest they think too much about themselves and too little about their mission. Career-management plans help this happen: high-echelon bureau people wanting to get ahead must travel widely through the bureau's bailiwick, learning the politics of an agency's holding its own, and discovering the Parkinson's Laws that make the world safe for bureaucracy. This may be great for careers. If the career is one in land management, it bodes ill for the land. The rising careerist has too little time to travel widely at Concord, as Thoreau did, or to understand what Aldo Leopold considered the outstanding scientific discovery of the twentieth century—the complexity of the land organism. "If the land mechanism as a whole is good," he said, "then every part is good, whether we understand it or not. If the biota, in the course of aeons, has built something we like but do not understand, then who but a fool would discard seemingly useless parts? To keep every cog and wheel is the first precaution of intelligent tinkering."

For its first whole century, the AMC made a career of learning about the cogs and wheels of the White Mountains. For a slightly shorter span, an individual did the same thing, and never underestimate Individual Power. Drawing upon his experience as a planner and AMC climber (1908-1910), Benton MacKaye became a legend in his own time, in the appraisal of Paul Oehser, of the Smithsonian. Benton "was forever young in heart, and eternally grateful for the privilege of living so long in the best world that he knew of, imperfect though it was." He was old enough to vote at the turn of the century, but just before voting conceived of an Appalachian Trail, presenting the idea comprehensively in 1921. The trail was to be much more than a long path through wild mountains. He saw it as "the backbone of a primeval environment, a sort of refuge from civilization which was becoming too mechanized." He wanted clusters of parks around this backbone, and a network of trails planned to intersect at strategic points with railroads. He liked the idea of triangle vacations: train to trail to train to home.

What Benton MacKaye called the crassitudes of civilization— billboard, pavement, or auto horn—were negations of the wilderness, itself "the perfect norm, wild and untouched land as distinguished from domesticated cornfield, pasture, or farm woodlot." Wilderness was the product of paleontology, a reservoir of stored experience in the ways of life before man. He urged: "We must win back our wilderness because we are losing it. We have upset the balance of the . . . 'Big Three' states of living (primeval, agrarian, industrial) . . . there should be room enough for all— both for the gregariously minded folks who like parks and playgrounds, and for the solitary-minded who seek the lonely shores."

Like Johnson and Muir, he wanted to organize to defend wilderness, and became one of the founders of The Wilderness Society, advocating at the time that "any body of people coming together for a purpose (whatever it may be) should consist of persons wholly wedded to that purpose and should consist of nobody else. If the purpose be Cannibalism . . . then 'nobody but a Cannibal should be admitted. There should be plenty of discussion and disagreement as to how and the means, but none whatever as to the ends."

He wanted each member of the Society, in each locality, to find some local job to do—a variation of his Appalachian Trail program of local groups' voluntarily building and taking care of their own sections of the trail, bringing many into enjoyable and useful activity. He also proposed a series of ecological study areas throughout the continent to represent the several natural communities in each of them, and in 1935 proposed that there be a national wilderness system. In December 1975, a few days before he died, Benton MacKaye thanked Stuart Chase for an article calling attention to the world-wide devastation of forest lands, and added, "It is the same old story which led me into forestry under Gifford Pinchot seventy years ago last June."

The hills of home had found their match, and tributes to him fill half of the March 1976 *The Living Wilderness*. One of the most moving is Lewis Mumford's about a man, an idea, and the difference they made together. Mumford first visited Benton's home in Shirley Center in the spring of 1929. "What surprised me there," he wrote, "is what surprised me in Thoreau's Concord: that such a passionate love for the natural landscape in its most rugged moments could have been nourished in an environment so mild and gentle, with rolling meadows and patches of woodland and marshland . . . and a distant glimpse of the far-from-overpowering heights of Wachusett. The whole countryside seemed but one step away from complete cultivation and domestication." Perhaps that very fact, Mumford thought, may have encouraged young MacKaye to deeper exploration.

Like Thoreau, MacKaye appreciated the communal values of New England villages, and even better than Thoreau, the culture of cities. "So far from believing that man's three major environments, the primeval, the rural, and the communal or urban, were mutually exclusive, MacKaye held rather that they were complementary, and all three were necessary for man's full development. . . . If one part of MacKaye was attached to the rehabilitation of indigenous American values, he was equally concerned to develop a global strategy favorable to the maintenance of similar values in other habitats and cultures."

One indigenous value his Appalachian Trail awaits the rehabilitation of is the railroads. The White Mountain section of the trail itself was completed in 1932, when railroads still went to little places, with the marking of the existing trails then managed by the AMC and the Dartmouth Outing Club, the Maine Appalachian Trail Club agreeing to continue the trail to Mount Katahdin. In 1938 the National Park Service and Forest Service established the Appalachian Trailway, a zone two miles wide along the trail to be free of motor transport or any development incompatible with recreational uses of the trail. Myron Avery, with Arthur Perkins, inherited MacKaye's idea and had led in the task of connecting it with the earth. In 1952 Avery declared at a meeting of the Appalachian Trail Conference that the Maine to Georgia trail was complete. Congress, in 1968, passed the National Trail System legislation introduced in 1964 by Senator

Gaylord Nelson, and the Appalachian Trail was recognized in federal law. We now suggest that the Army Corps of Engineers, who are very effective in these matters, be persuaded to leave wild rivers in their courses and get tired railroads back on the track. This would rescue Benton MacKaye's original idea.

Whatever the origins of protection, the White Mountains continue to fare well thanks to several groups whose combined energies insure that good management does not stop at artificial boundaries, whether of national parks, national forests, state lands, or private lands. Many conservation groups not already engaged in management are partly equipped to do so, and, as Tom Deans and Ken Olson suggest, may well extend their capability as they realize that the survival of wilderness depends on husbandry as well as advocacy. It also depends upon the generosity of its beneficiaries. Institutions that put the public weal before private gain are customarily endowed well. Wilderness deserves such support too, and the opportunity to endow the open university of wilderness is impressive. To help realize it, funds need to be channeled into organizations like the Appalachian Trail Conference, the Nature Conservancy, the Sierra Club, the Trust for Public Land, The Wilderness Society, and of course the Appalachian Mountain Club and Friends of the Earth. Such funds can most appropriately come from the people who now enjoy wild places, or have enjoyed them, or would like Frederick Law Olmsted's uncounted millions to enjoy them. Current contributions and last gifts can mean a lasting wilderness.

Wilderness is what the White Mountains had, but lost. The once vast area in which the web of life perfected itself with no assistance from bureaus or technology has been severed and severed again. The species that were lost in that severing are ended. We shall never know what they might have meant to their surroundings or to us. Beautiful pockets of wildness nonetheless remain and some might almost grow back together again. Tomorrow's White Mountain restoration, to all but the most discerning, could be indistinguishable from the original. For this to happen, however, the mountains cannot be periodically disrupted by dam and road building, mining and quarrying, logging and clearing, and by recreational excesses and the pervasive effects of pollution of the surrounding air. Glaciers, of course, could unpave the way toward recovery, especially if they were once again to be two thousand feet deeper than Mount Washington is high; but no one is urging so drastic a remedial step.

Various courses lie open to public and private organizations in managing people so as to hasten the healing without expediting the arrival of 1984 in wild places. These places can be hurt by those who love them. It will ease the damage, when it threatens to be severe, to push access points back a bit so that the wheel does less work and the foot does more. If wilderness must be rationed, those who are willing to earn it should be favored. This is Garrett Hardin's point, and he makes it knowing that it rules him out. Paul Brooks perceives another kind of rationing: "If you are in a canoe traveling at three miles an hour, the lake on which you are paddling is ten times as long and ten times as broad as it is to the man in a speedboat going thirty. . . . More people can use the same space with the same results." So speed limits are in order. Other limits may be in time, such as those river travelers observe in the Grand Canyon; they are required to take out everything they bring in except urine. The successive steps needed to reduce human impact on wilderness surely increase the impact upon the freedom that wilderness was able to grant when the world was less crowded. Those limits do mean, however, that when the visitor has gone, the wilderness is still there, not smothered in an embrace, but essentially intact.

Impact that might otherwise be ubiquitous is concentrated by the judicious placing of huts, as the AMC has demonstrated. But a hut has a basic drawback. Move a hut in, and wildness pulls back, in fact and in spirit. The hut user shares the problem of the woman in Samivel's cartoon who could enjoy solitude more if it were only less lonely.

The impact most serious of all comes from there being too few people—too few who know a given place, who have learned to understand and love it, and thus are prepared to protect it. Glen Canyon was the place no one knew, and it is gone. No visitor impact can compete with a dam, a chainsaw, or a bulldozer—or, for that matter, the impact of acid rain or radioactive fallout. The AMC huts, like Sierra Club wilderness outings, have built battalions of people who care. Without those people, there might have been no solitude at all. Be grateful, if you will, for their own special love for the mountain or shore of their home country, for their speaking in behalf of high-rimmed valleys and of views from summits, of whole forests and free streams, of nonhuman denizens and of human visitors too, and human needs far into the future. They are in the tradition of the Olmsteds, the Thoreaus, the Muirs, the MacKayes, the Leopolds—a tradition to keep alive if wildness is to remain the preservation of the world Thoreau believed it to be.

Otherwise progress as presently misconstrued will erase the last vestige of original America. How fast it has gone! A mere one hundred thirty years ago, when oil was first discovered in Pennsylvania and John Muir was nine years old, Thoreau wrote: "I am reminded by my journey how exceedingly new this country still is. . . . We live only on the shores of a continent even yet, and hardly know where the rivers come from which float our navy. The very timber and boards and shingles of which our houses are made, grew but yesterday in a wilderness where the Indian still hunts and the moose runs wild."

Thirty years later, the AMC was born. Three more, Benton MacKaye. Add thirteen, the Sierra Club. Twice as many more, and World War I was over; an epidemic of Spanish influenza was followed by one of automobiles. Another eleven, and a world half as populous as today's entered the Great Depression. A second World War came within a decade, and its end marked the beginning of the atomic age and the race for ever grosser national products. The earth grew no larger.

For fifty years big wilderness has been disappearing at the rate of a million acres a year in the national forests, and still more has disappeared outside the forests. Other wildness may go too—the most remarkable wild heritage of all, DNA. In the last five years the urge was born to second-guess a force that has been created, honed, and perfected in wilderness for three and a half thousand million years. A trace of its first day on earth is still alive in today's wilderness, and in each of us.

Given another decade or two, humanity could quite handily erase the last of the earth's wilderness. Or it could heed Aldo Leopold's warning: "When the last corner lot is covered with tenements we can still make a playground by tearing them down, but when the last antelope goes by the board, not all the playground associations in Christendom can do aught to replace the loss." For as Wallace Stegner has said, "It is not given to man to create wilderness. But he can make deserts, and has."

We could pledge never to tell tomorrow's children what they missed, or we could take a new look at progress and continue only that kind that avoids the mindless growth that destroys its feedstock. Surely we can let the wildness that still is still be. We can go back where we ravaged, and restore, if we try soon enough. We can, upright people that we are, rediscover the foot; we can save a place to walk in, and an antelope too. Every child who is there on the first day of our tercentennary still has a chance, through us, to wake up in an America that is still spacious, still beautiful, still wild enough in places. Wilder, perhaps, than it now is in New England's oldest climax, these, the White Mountains of home.

DAVID R. BROWER, *President*
Friends of the Earth
June 5, 1978   *and Honorary Member, AMC*

Acknowledgments

O F THE THIRTY-TWO volumes so far published in this format under the same general editor, all have been profoundly influenced by the artistry of Ansel Adams, Nancy Newhall, and Eliot Porter, and most of them have been published to rally support for endangered places. This one recognizes support already given, primarily by the Appalachian Mountain Club, to what we should like to have called the oldest range, had mountains in Canada and Greenland not claimed to be older. In any event, the AMC is the oldest club, having passed its century mark in 1976, and we are grateful for the efforts of four consecutive AMC presidents who reigned over the book's formative years—John Perry, Bill King, Ruby Horwood, and Andy Nichols. Continuous faith during this period was kept by Philip Levin, editor, then editor emeritus, of *Appalachia*, who as Ken Olson puts it, "sustained and prodded us, reasoned with those who thought the book a fanciful idea, and incited us with visions about how a beautifully done volume might contribute to people's appreciation of wilderness."

The roster of people in and out of the AMC and Forest Service who encouraged Phil Levin and assisted Ken Olson in his part of the book is a long one. We are greatful for the essential elements all of them have added to the whole for so long. It was nine years ago that Ken and Tom Deans thought there should be a book, and seven years ago that Amory Lovins met Ken and thought it should be a book like this one; he had just finished such a book for Friends of the Earth about the mountains of Wales. Books of this magnitude have caused hesitation before and did so this time too. Reasonable people are likely to wonder whether a commitment to spend more than one hundred thousand dollars on a project will lead to a corresponding commitment on the part of readers to rescue the commitment. Through the good work of members of the AMC Council and Board of Publications, the New York Graphic Society offered substantial support, for which we are particularly grateful to Tim Hill. But the project still required someone to take the full financial and editorial responsibility, lest the printers give up hope. The book was not quite ready to fly.

It was waiting, it seems, for Harvard. Brooks Atkinson ('17) wrote a book in his youth that Stephen Lyons ('76) discovered in his. Alfred Knopf had originally seen in that book a flavor of White Mountain experience that Steve believed would complement beautifully what we had in hand. It had appeared in a limited edition and for unknown reasons enjoyed a still more limited sale. Steve met with Mr. Atkinson and gained his approval of the condensation he hoped for. He then pored through libraries, east and west, as well as through Karl Wendelowski's previous poring. Out of this came the textual counterpoint to what Brooks Atkinson had experienced in the twenties, Ken Olson in the seventies, and Benton MacKaye before the turn of the century, when he conceived of the Appalachian Trail (and later of a global wilderness system.)

Special thanks are due Ken Olson and George DeWolfe for their patience as they gave up time but not hope; to Amory Lovins, who took time out from devising soft energy paths for the world to encourage the work and to photograph White Mountains as well; to Philip Evans, who brought a special gift of seeing from his home mountains of Wales to these of New England, then followed through to help his friends at Mondadori recapture what he had photographed; and to Steve Lyons, who took on the editorial task and more, bringing together text, excerpt, and illustration so that they achieve together what none could alone, and doing all this with consummate skill.

Let no one forget, however, what Benton MacKaye, the Forest Service, and the Appalachian Mountain Club achieved preeminently in keeping the subject of this book as intact as it is, or underestimate what you, their successors, can do to keep it that way for another generation or two. The battle to save places can never be won, but reprieves can be renewed. One good turn deserves another, and several organizations stand ready to help you take yours. Please do.   —D.R.B.

New England's White Mountains

Whatever the reasons, the White Mountains, for me as a child, always lay in sunlight, on the other side of night. Now that I know the golden light of evening on my own acres in the shadow of these mountains, the golden light that falls like a benediction on shorn fields and great barn of slivered gray and old white house and low walls of stone, I have very other recurrent memories of them, but none that can wholly blot out those visualizations of childhood. That evening light brings a rest to the spirit that stimulant sunlight cannot give, that evening light eases and consoles and blesses, as Handel's "Largo" does, and Wordsworth's "Cuckoo" and Redfield's cedared lanes on hillsides deep with snow.

Even as a child my heart homed north. I liked the moan of winter wind as I lay warm in bed. I liked the noise of sleet and gritty snow on the window glass. In the red sunsets beyond the black bars of winter woods I knew an uplift of the heart that came to me from no other of the year's sunsets. I liked the snugness of stable and greenhouse and house on winter nights. My kinship with horses and cow and hens never seemed so close as then. The friendliness of my dog was never so manifest as when we two stopped in woods, on some still evening of intense cold in February, to watch screech owl or hiding hawk. Then he snuggled up to me for warmth and companionship. Cold and wildness out of doors were bracing to the hardy youngster I was. I liked snow in the face, and buffeting wind, and the stimulation of low temperature. Indoors I loved the·sense of warmth and comfort and protection and safety that was accented so sharply by the wildness and cold without.

I had no foreknowledge as a child, or intimation, or dream, that I should live in later years summer after summer in New Hampshire; that I should own a little share of the Granite State, and learn to know my way about it, and the ways of its people, almost as well as I knew the countryside and people of Pennsylvania. Once fabled, and almost fabulous, those White Mountains are old acquaintances now, long lived with and long loved, a part of me for as long as I shall be. . . .

— CORNELIUS WEYGANDT

AT HOME IN THE WILD

Every climber knows how these terraces are found where the strata are favourable, and is familiar with their aspect and their technical importance, which is often decisive. They can be valuable allies, allowing you to traverse freely across the face of the cliffs, to avoid impassable or over-difficult steps, and by clever flanking movements, sometimes very wide, to spy out the weak points which leads to victory. In mountain climbing the vertical must be the dominant interest, and lateral digressions arise only from necessity. "Straight for it," is the usual phrase, "we can play about another time!" In critical moments, one is thankful for their help, with no more than a rapid glance for getting direction. Their study is reserved for the mountaineer's leisure moments; the peakbagger has no time for them. But when we lie on some quiet height, in happy forgetfulness of time and purpose and the call of success, half-dreaming, half-observant, reasoning almost unconsciously within ourselves; when in such solemn hours of idleness, which often tell us more than can the fleeting happiness of victory, we look around upon the illummined ridges and into the shadows of their most hidden folds, with eye, ear and mind alike busy, then these terraces begin to confide gently to us of their whence and whither, and to reveal the whole charm and eternal sublimity of those secret pathways which lead to the inntermost heart of the mountains.

—JULIUS KUGY

Introduction

MAN'S work is visible from almost any summit in the White Mountains. Fire towers, old and new logging roads, ski lifts, alpine slides, summit houses and other structures claim several mountainsides in the region. Crowded into the valleys are town after town. In an earlier day many of them would have qualified as New England villages. Some still do, but most have taken on the character of the cities. The mountains are now bounded south, east, and west by neon communities like those which clutter the rim of any American city: fish fry and pizza joints, the world's best coffee, golden arches, have it your way. A millennium from now, inheritors of this place who dig here for our spoor will find not marble and monoliths but unweathered plastic. Boston has nibbled its way north to the White Mountains, is getting into the seams, and, if the trend continues, will soon gnaw through, infecting the country north of the mountains with the well known disease of sameness. At the behest of real estate enterprisers we will have made an island of the only federally owned backcountry in New Hampshire, the White Mountain National Forest.

In the recent history of the New Hampshire mountains, there has scarcely been a period when the fates of men and wilderness have not been intermingled. Prior to the mid-eighteenth century, the White Mountains had been an effective natural barrier against human intrusion from the south. Wilderness had always frightened men, and none entered it unless driven by good reason. Even more alarming to would-be settlers was the long-lived threat of death at the hands of the French and Indians. By the time Quebec fell in 1760, the population in the colony of New Hampshire had swelled enough to warrant northward expansion. From then until the outbreak of the American Revolution, colonists advanced the New England frontier as far as the southern White Mountains, while a few hardies circumnavigated the central ranges and built homes in the upper reaches of the Androscoggin Valley. In the north, the Connecticut Lakes region went unsettled until after 1812, by which time industrialism had rooted in the foothills of southern New Hampshire.

Rivers rising in the White Mountains provided power, and along them industrial towns grew up and thrived. Textile manufacture and, later, shoe production underpinned the state's economy as more citizens were drawn to riverine portions of the state. Soon the interior population surpassed the aggregate populations of the coastal towns. In 1838 railroad tracks reached Nashua, a community near the Massachusetts border, and New Hampshire's rail era began in earnest. Over six hundred miles of track was laid by the time the Civil War broke out. The railroad meant inexpensive shipping costs for producers lucky enough to be near the lines. For remote farmers and commodity producers, though, the railroad spelled irreversible economic decline, a process that had begun earlier when the Erie Canal was completed. Shipping via the canal cost producers five dollars instead of the usual one hundred dollars per ton, making it cheaper for western producers to provide for eastern needs. Unable to compete, most of New Hampshire's hill farmers gave up their rock-strewn lands to flintier folks. They too eventually left, and by the eighteen sixties most towns had lost population. Some people migrated west. Others remained in New Hampshire, choosing to live in river towns, where industry was salvation. Over forty percent of New Hampshire was farmland then. By 1900 the figure was less than twenty percent, and by mid-century seven percent. The forest, left to its own devices, had reclaimed the land.

What wilderness the farmers did not subdue fell to the loggers. Nearly all New England succumbed, over time, to the woodsman's ax. Prior to the Revolution, the region's white pines, the most majestic of eastern trees (save, perhaps, the disease-doomed American elm), were blazed with the King's broad arrow, then cut and shipped to England, where they became masts for the British navy. After Independence, our new government assiduously tried not to emulate the excesses of the country from which it had just freed itself. Nevertheless, in the spirit of democracy and with faith in private enterprise, our government sold most of New England.

The public domain became the private domain of logging interests which, even as late as the mid-eighteen hundreds, paid as little as twelve-and-a-half cents per acre for millions of acres. The timber rape proceeded apace. Loggers went where farmers never could, into the heartland of the big mountains. They cut roads into deep stands of virgin timber, angling them up and around even the higher summits. Horses and oxen twitched out the big logs. The logging companies cut rail lanes and laid track into the mountain wilderness and removed the booty on steam-driven trains. Clearcutting was the practice of the day, though much of what was cut was left as slash, an inexcusable waste. The desiccated remains of a once vital forest lay about like so much tinder. Several enormous fires ripped through the cut over lands and consumed uncut trees as well. Often as not, it was the cinder-belching steam engine—the "puffin' devil"—whose hot sparks ignited the wilderness. Mountain streams became clogged with debris, the life literally choked out of them. No vegetation grew on the blackened land, so rain falling in the burned White Mountains flowed unchecked into the headwaters of streams that fed New Hampshire's industrial towns. Heavy floods struck the lowlands, hurting industry. Finally, an odd-bedfellows alliance of industrialists and conservationists prodded the federal government into acting to stop the abuses of private loggers.

The White Mountain National Forest was born of the prodding. Lands were purchased by the government under the provisions of the Weeks Law, passed in 1911. The Law gave the government the right to protect the headwaters of navigable waterways by committing contiguous lands to the public domain. By 1918 great parcels of White Mountain backcountry had been returned to federal ownership, much of it bought back at $7.50 an acre. The buying-back process continues today. Had private enterprise husbanded rather than raided the resources, we would most likely have no White Mountain National Forest.

The Forest that has been given into the public trust is a small one, about 730,000 acres, and is what is commonly described as "second growth," not virgin. It is neither large nor primeval because of the historical forces that shaped it. The east was settled first, and, logically enough, the raid on America's natural resources began here. Now the east must pay the price for its haste to achieve dominion over the wilderness. Although nature's immutable processes have restored the land to another order of matchless natural beauty, we must now observe that beauty as an anomaly rather than as the canon. What we have taken pains to preserve is a vivid but tiny and poignant reminder of what the whole once looked like. The White Mountains are five times, maybe ten times, larger than what we have isolated and protected as National Forest. If by some temporal alchemy we were able to recast history—if, for example, our forebears had landed first on the west coast and then expanded eastward—much of New England might now be a National Park.

But the moving finger writes, and we cannot lure it back to cancel half a line. Instead, we should learn to do what the economists only profess: to value what is scarce. Precisely because there is no vast quasi-western wilderness here, every parcel of remaining backcountry is that much rarer and more in need of protection.

ALLEN H. BENT wrote this in his *Bibliography of the White Mountains* (1911): "The White Mountains . . . have had more written about them, probably, than any other mountains, the Alps alone excepted." Whether or not that is still true today remains for some enterprising bibliographer to determine; regardless, a circle of mostly eastern writers has conferred on this range a kind of literary immortality. We owe thanks in good measure to Hawthorne for his stories of the White Hills, especially for "The Great Stone Face" and "The Ambitious Guest." Longfellow and Whittier also contributed, and Whittier's lifelong friend, the poetess Lucy Larcom. Francis Parkman wrote about the Whites as did the well-known ministers Manasseh Cutler, Henry Ward Beecher and Thomas Starr King, the bot-

anist Asa Gray, the scientist Louis Agazziz, the navigator Nathaniel Bowditch, and the journalists William Cullen Bryant and William Ellery Channing. Brooks Atkinson, coauthor of this book, has written of these mountains, as has Justice William O. Douglas and Edmund Ware Smith. Robert Frost and T. S. Eliot, too, have committed to verse some of their interpretations of the range. And Thoreau himself, who went twice to the Whites, wrote on his experiences.

We owe thanks also to the early artists who caught on canvas The Range That Was. The White Mountain School, our first native school of art, flourished in North Conway, New Hampshire. Its practitioners, painters like Thomas Cole and Thomas Doughty, later became the leaders of the Hudson River School. J. F. Kensett, A. B. Durand, B. G. Stone, Benjamin Champney painted here, as did George Inness and Albert Bierstadt, among others. Today in the Mount Washington Valley, a community of artists is once again at work interpreting mountains.

It may justifiably be asked why a mountain range with such a prodigious cultural legacy needs once again to be interpreted in print. No easy answer exists. Because the White Mountains are visited by so many people who know them intimately, and because, as the old saw goes, familiarity breeds contempt, it is tempting to suggest that the mountains need a beautiful book which will turn people away from contempt and toward awe. That is, I think, a cynic's view. Lovers of eastern wilderness are not so callous. And the heartland of the White Mountains, the National Forest itself, is not about to be debased by crude logging practices or outrageous roadbuilding policies; nor is it under imminent threat of development. Still, there is cause for concern. We ourselves and our official stewards, the federal and state agencies, have conceded too early that government and its private contractors are the fittest keepers of the backcountries we have fought to preserve. If there is a message in this book—other than the timeless one that beauty and peace surround us and are close by for our discovery and rediscovery—it is this: Our last wildernesses will not survive without both advocates and stewards. The battle to preserve vestiges of natural America will not be won simply by inscribing lines around what we have "saved" and entrusting government to do the rest. Husbandry by the citizens themselves is the second front of conservation.

New England's White Mountains is foremost a visual feast. Philip Evans, a British photographer, does what is unquestionably the finest color photography ever to be undertaken in the White Mountains. His vision is fresh, his rendering singular. His cophotographer, Amory Lovins, is a master of forest detail in color. And George DeWolfe is probably the most original black-and-white photographer of these hills since Guy Shorey. To complement their work, David Brower has chosen to republish Brooks Atkinson's delightful book, *Skyline Promenades*, first out in 1925. I am honored to collaborate with these artists. We five of us, with Dave's guidance and that of the book's editor, Stephen Lyons, have tried to assemble in one volume a sort of mountain anthology. The photography may be viewed by itself, the essays read independently or in sequence, or the whole book experienced. We have made no attempt to present the White Mountain wilderness in all its aspects—only to include, rather eclectically, what the other literature of these hills has not. Still, a thread runs through the writing. As you hike across the White Mountain skyline with Brooks Atkinson and his companion Pierre, the other essays, in sequence, take you from pre-history to the future. No man's eye witnessed the making of any wilderness, but many men's energies will be necessary to guarantee its perpetuity.

READING about mountains is no real substitute for going there, but it may be the next best thing. There are parallels enough between the two enterprises. You can climb vicariously as you read and can appreciate the visual feast that is wilderness as you pore over superb photography. As you do this you will do well to remember John Muir's words, written about the Sierra but applicable to any mountain range: "No amount of word-making will ever make a single soul to *know* these mountains. As well seek to warm the naked by lectures on caloric and pictures of flame. One day's exposure to the mountains is better than cartloads of books. See how willingly Nature poses herself upon photographer's plates. No earthly chemicals are so sensitive as those of the human soul. All that is required is exposure, and purity of soul."

For my own part, I have tried, while writing, to remember Muir's words. If occasionally they escaped me, I quietly pled guilty to confusing symbol for reality and sentenced myself to this dose from Stearns Morse's and John Anderson's *The Book of the White Mountains*: "There is much to be said for such tourists as one who exclaimed, on entering Michelangelo's chapel for the Medici, 'Pretty good,' and went away again. This is the essence of the shrewdest criticism in the face of masterpiece, even if it does raise the assumption that the truly sensitive tourist is the one who doesn't write a book on the White Mountains."

To stand on a summit, to look, and not to touch what you see— a circumstance forced on all wingless creatures who climb moun- tains—is enlightened greed. You possess what you see and are enriched by the vision. You can assimilate the land, interpret it as you wish, hoard it with your eyes. Do all that and you still leave the wilderness unaltered for those who will follow you. That is a harmless form of realty. I have bought much land this way and have even put in a bid on the Atlantic, which lies eighty miles east of Mt. Washington On a sparkling morning you might see it from the summit. You must look twice, though, even three times, to assure yourself that the sleek silver eel your eye has seized on really is the ocean.

Inland, two things strike you: the concentrism of the sur- rounding mountains and their physical economy. Peaks are scat- tered about like stars in a compact galaxy. Valleys are mere dips and ridges just ripples that curve away to a land which flattens beyond sight. The horizon seems to droop at either end. Whether this is a trick your eyes play on you I cannot say. But I go heady in the viewing, which, after all, is a wilderness man's great delight.

During our brief tenure here we have so completely altered New England's wilds that we will never again enjoy a landscape wholly free of human interference. Yet nature's restorative pow- ers have enabled the fallen eastern wilderness to recover, and the growing reverence for nature gives reason to hope those lands will remain healthy. It's important that they do so, for too many people have not yet had the chance to benefit from clear streams, unpeopled valleys and untamed mountains. We can never again know the original American landscape, but by caring and working hard—not only in New England, but also across this and other continents—we can preserve the vestiges of wildness. We owe that much to the future citizens of this planet.

I commend to you, in the reading and the viewing, and in the land itself, a once and future wilderness.

W. KENT OLSON

New Haven, Connecticut
March 1978

Drawn by I. Sprague.

B. W. Thayer & Co. Lith.

THE NOTCH OF THE WHITE MOUNTAINS, WITH THE WILLEY HOUSE.

Oakes' White Mountain Scenery, Plate 3.

Entered according to act of Congress in the year 1848 by W. Oakes, in the Clerk's office of the District Court of Massachusetts.

24]

The Lay of the Land

OVER six hundred million years ago, when North America and Africa were one continent, there was no Atlantic Ocean, nor any mountains on what is now our eastern seaboard. Great oceans surrounded the merged continents, which over eons split and drifted apart on the earth's fluid mantle. Into the opening between these plates the ancestral Atlantic flowed, disappearing later as the continents joined again. Their slow forceful collision, with its attendant heat and incalculable pressures, made mountains—the ancient Appalachians. The continents drifted once more and the modern Atlantic flowed in. Over two hundred million years of erosion have worn this old range to its roots.

But even before that wearing process was fully underway, another range had begun to form. The new Appalachians grew of sediments deposited west of the old range by the ancestral Atlantic, and by eonic upwellings of molten rock—magma—which fairly lifted this lesser range into the sky. Under continued pressure, from which nothing was immune, the land went plastic, its liquefaction the result of great geologic hiccups. More magma rose. Streams and the inland sea pared away the land as hot pliant rock continued to rise from eight to nine miles below the earth's surface.

The wearing down exceeded the welling up, but for all that was carted away the bedrock remained, forever rising, shoving the inland waters eastward with every cant. Freshwater runoff from the higher bumps chiseled the land and quickened with each steepening cut. Streams carved Vs in the high rolling surfaces that would become Bigelow Lawn, the Alpine Garden and the Gulfside Ridge. Something like the present White Mountains of New Hampshire came of this aqueous sculpting.

Nearly two million years ago—a mere instant in geologic time—a process began which gave the White Mountains the character they have today. What had been a warm climate became cooler. The mean annual temperature dropped only a few degrees, but that was enough of a change to begin an ice age. No human eye witnessed what happened to the White Mountains, but we can imagine what man might have seen had he been there. . . .

Glaciers predominate the landscape. Dry snow robs water from the air, moisture that in a fairer climate would find its way back to the ocean. Snow building on itself compresses the lower tiers into a gelid mass that under continued pressure fails to support the load. And the whole thing moves.

Winds from the west prevail on Mt. Washington. They lift snow from the western flank and the narrow gullies of rivers like the Ammonoosuc, and carry them eastward for a second drop in the equally featureless valleys of the Dry, Cutler, Ellis and Peabody, where the snow, in the lee, is protected from further removal. High in each eastern river course, snow accumulates and begets an alpine glacier, whose weight carries it downward, taking pieces of the mountain with it. Each glacier scrabbles up loose rocks as it moves, grinding them along underneath. Crevasses on the upper surfaces accept melt-water, which percolates downward and freezes in rock joints and foliations, popping apart rocks and ledges. But the big work is the making of vast natural bowls. Inching forward, the dense ice cleaves whole rock faces from the mountainsides. Pluck, Tuckerman, a fine symmetrical ravine. Pluck, Huntington, craggy and good for climbers. Pluck, the Great Gulf, a steep cul-de-sac with a half dozen smaller ravines contributing to the main one.

Temperatures cool enough to excite local glaciers have grander effects in Labrador, where snow and ice are amassing. So large is the growth that the snows assimilate whole glaciers. Several merge to form a single ice sheet that, as it crawls in all directions, enlarges to continental dimensions. Its movement south through Canada is slow, perhaps three or four feet a year, but inexorable. The glacial wall is not uniform but lobed; amoebic, it advances podia. The ever broadening front creeps south to upper New Hampshire. Colloidal snouts follow riverbeds, nose into notches, ride part way up hillsides. They are not yet large enough to surmount peaks, but the sheet builds as it goes, fed by more snow in the Laurentian uplands. It is a river flowing over itself, now nearly as deep as the surrounding peaks are high, and still rising. As the valleys fill, the ice sheet takes for the summits, braiding around the highest peaks, making temporary islands of them. Finally, they disappear altogether. Mt. Washington lies buried under a thousand feet or more of blue and white ice. Gone are the summits, gone even the suggestion of mountains: hardly a bump is left on a snowscape as flat as the Antarctican plateaus.

Though encased in a moving continent of ice, the mountains are quite stable. The southward flow tears at bedrock, having its greatest success in the notches. In Pinkham, Dixville, Carter, Franconia, Crawford, Zealand and the others, the glacier digs away sidewalls and valley bottoms, rounding each V into a U. High up, the icework gentles the western and northern slopes of the big mountains, makes the southern and eastern sides more precipitous. It cleaves the eastern edges of Monroe and the southern Presidentials, giving them cornices. The ice cuts passages through which water will fall during the thaw: Crystal Cascade, Glen Ellis Falls, Thoreau Falls and many others. It digs two hollows at five thousand feet: Lakes of the Clouds. Dirt and vegetation are carried oceanward by subglacial streams.

A slight rise in temperature is enough to stop a glacier; as soon as melt exceeds build-up, the wall retreats. So it is with the ice sheet, which comes and goes *four times* in 2,000,000 years. The last flow and ebb, the "Wisconsin Stage," is a cycle of 50,000 years, more than half spent in recession. At its scalloped southern edge—some two thousand miles from its source—the front deposits most of Long Island, Nantucket, Martha's Vineyard and, as an afterthought, Cape Cod. Under uncountable tons of ice, northeastern America sinks a few hundred feet. The Atlantic, having given up so much water to the ice sheet, is also low, but it rises more rapidly with glacial melt than does the land. For a time southern New Hampshire's coast lies under water, and much of Maine's. The fattened St. Lawrence is an ocean extension that hooks down into Vermont. The receding glacier leaves sandy outwashes, glacial till, broken rock.

It is a stuttering retreat at best. Capricious temperature changes cause reformation and quick advance, then equally sudden melting. New Hampshire gets all of its lakes, some scoured, others formed by the weight of ice chunks sheared, then abandoned.

Rivers flow under the stagnant ice, only to be glutted by shorn rock that forms serpentine ridges—eskers—in the glacial path. New Hampshire's valleys bulge with water at the withering edges of glacial tongues. The lateral runoff cuts terraces in the Zealand Valley, among other places, and pushes sand into the bottomlands—the Saco Intervale. Neighboring Vermont gets—gift of gifts—a whale trapped inland as the land rises. The ice sheet is gone.

FROM immediate post-glacial times to nearly twenty centuries after the birth of Christ is a flickering of twelve to fifteen thousand years. But it is time enough for many changes. Trees return, mixed hardwood and conifers to the lowlands and diminutive twisted krummholz up high. The climate assumes some consistency, and a timberline settles at 4500 feet. Tiny flora, including some arctic genera, claim eight square miles or so of alpine tundra. Frost fractures the blocks of gneiss, making talus slopes and talus stripes, frost terraces and scree piles. Rivers and pebbles carve potholes and round out the rough work of the ice. Tarns and bogs form, and ecosystems succeed one another, making soil in the process.

There is time enough for Indians to build eastern nations, name mountains, and succumb to white men. Enterprisers strip the land bald, governments buy it back, and enlightened men try to conserve it. Geologists postulate that the most recent ice sheet may not have been the last, and that we may be enjoying an interlude between glaciers in this, the land of microseconds and millennia.

This is but a rough sketch of the geological history whose details still escape even the experts. But ordinary New Hampshire folks have known the outlines of the history for years. Newcomers to the mountains often ask, "How did all these rocks get on Mount Washington?" And it's a pipe-smoking, hardscrabble Yankee who answers, "The glacier brought 'em, of course." The city man thinks on this a moment and says, "And what happened to the glacier?" "Why," says the old man, with a wink, "it's gone back for another load."

One night, when he [the Indian] had laid down his coal, and seen a warm fire spring up therefrom, with a blinding smoke, a loud voice came out of the flame, and a great noise, like thunder, filled the air; and there rose up a vast pile of broken rocks. Out of the cloud resting on top came numerous streams, dancing down, foaming cold; and the voice spake to the astonished red hunter, saying, "Here the Great Spirit shall dwell, and watch over his favorite children."

—JOHN H. SPAULDING
Historical Relics of the White Mountains (1855)

I recollect a number of years ago, when quite a boy, some persons had been up in the hills and they said they had found a golden treasure, or carbuncle, which they said was under a large shelving rock and would be difficult to obtain for they might fall and be dashed to pieces. Moreover, they thought it was guarded by an evil spirit, supposing that it had been placed there by the Indians, and that they had killed one of their number and left him to guard the treasure, which some credulous, superstitious believed, and they got my father to engage to go search for it . . . but they could not find the place again, or anything that seemed to be like it, and worn out with fatigue and disappointment, they returned. Never since, to my knowledge, has anyone found that wonderful place again. or been troubled with the mountain spirit.

—ETHAN ALLEN CRAWFORD

Place of the Storm Spirit

*Ask them (the Indians) whither they go when they dye,
they will tell you, pointing with their finger to Heaven,
beyond the white mountains.*

—JOHN JOSSELYN (1674)

THE immortal hand or eye that framed New Hampshire cared little for symmetry. The state is an irregular triangle, its northern end a blunted vertex formed by the Connecticut River on the west and the Longfellow Mountains on the east. A hilly Vermont backcountry crowds it on one side, and a vast, if disturbed, Maine wilderness extends from the other. Way south the state goes wide and squat, and there is little to distinguish it from Massachusetts, which forms the southern border. A twenty-mile coastline is the state's only contact with the ocean. Holding roughly to the middle of the state and running northwesterly are the White Mountains. They spill at both ends into neighboring states, arriving as foothills in Vermont, continuing as mountains into Maine.

Settlers in the early 1600s kept pretty much to New Hampshire's coast, occupying what is now greater Portsmouth. The best farming was there, and fish and furs. The lowlands yielded abundant timber, and the port itself provided immediate access to commercial shipping lanes.

From the sea, the most prominent feature of New England is the inland mountain range. In his 1524 letter to the King of France, the Florentine navigator Verrazano wrote of "high mountains back inland, growing smaller toward the sea." Several subsequent maps showed the *montagnas*, and sailors like Samuel de Champlain later confirmed their existence. Christopher Levett cruised the coast beginning in 1623 and met some of the "salvages" who inhabited the coastline. According to Levett's 1628 account, the Indians told him of "a great mountain called the Christall hill, being as they say one hundred miles in the country, yet it is to be seen at the sea side, and there is no ship arrives in New England, either to the West so farre as Cape Cod, or to the East so farre as Monhiggen, but they see this mountaine the first land, if the weather be cleere."

The Christall hill, of course, was the peak we now call Mt. Washington. To the Indians it was known as Agiochook, and was thought to be the inviolate home of the Great Spirit. Because of the Indian's reverence for the mountain, it remained unclimbed until 1642. In that year, Darby Field, an Englishman (or Irishman, depending on which historian you trust), left Portsmouth by boat and sailed a short distance up the Maine coast and into the mouth of the Saco River. A canoe and walking journey of several days brought him to the village of Pequaket (now Fryeburg, Maine), home of the Sokokis, Abnaki Indians of the Algonquin tribe. Field persuaded a few of the Abnakis to accompany him farther into the wilderness. Most of them went to within eight miles of their destination and refused to go any closer to Agiochook; but Field was able to persuade two Indians to join him in the ascent.

Governor John Winthrop of Massachusetts chronicled Field's success: "They went divers times through the thick clouds for a good space, and within four miles of the top they had no clouds, but very cold. By the way, among the rocks, there were two ponds, one a blackish water and the other reddish. The top of all was plain about 60 feet square. On the north side there was such a precipice, as they could hardly discern the bottom. They had neither cloud nor wind on the top, and moderate heat. All the country about him seemed a level, except here and there a hill rising above the rest, but far beneath them. He saw to the north a great water which he judged to be 100 miles broad, but could see no land beyond it. The sea by Saco seemed as if had been within 20 miles. He also saw a sea to the eastward, which he judged to be the Gulf of Canada: He saw some great waters in parts to the westward which he judged to be the great lake which Canada River comes out of. He found there much Muscovy glass, they could rive out pieces 40 feet long and 7 or 8 broad. When he came back to the Indians, he found them drying themselves by the fire, for they had had a great tempest of wind and rain. About a month after he went again, with five or six of his company, then they had some wind on top, and some clouds above them which hid the sun. They brought some stones which they supposed had been some diamonds, but they were most crystal."

Those who followed Field into the wilderness did so not for

Clay   Washington   Monroe   Franklin   Pleasant

THE WHITE MOUNTAINS, FROM THE GIANT'S GRAVE, NEAR THE MOUNT WASHINGTON HOUSE

Oakes' White Mountain Scenery, Plate 1.

Entered according to act of Congress in the year 1848 by Wm Oakes in the Clerks Office of the District Court of Mass.

adventure but for exploitation. Field's shining rocks surely meant riches, and reports, allegedly from the Indians themselves, told of great carbuncles hidden deep in the wilderness. One group of entrepreneurs, lured by these reports, spent $1,500,000 in a vain search for gold in the upper Ammonoosuc Valley. But most exploiters came to the mountains for less greedy purposes: to build homes, clear farmlands, establish taverns. Theirs was a quiet sort of manifest destiny. Yet, slow as the white advance may have been, it spelled the dissolution of the Abnaki way of life and the division of the eastern wilderness.

THE Abnakis were a peaceful people who subsisted on fish and game, supplemented by small amounts of maize. Their leader Passaconaway was an easy sort whose chieftainship predated the arrival of the *Mayflower*. Although the Abnakis were friendly with their white neighbors, they skirmished endlessly with the Mohawks across the mountains in New York. The fighting took its toll, as did pestilence, so that by the time Christopher Levett met Passaconaway in 1623, the Abnaki population had been reduced over twenty years from several thousand to a few hundred.

The chief treated white settlers deferentially, granting them large tracts of land, surrendering his tribe's guns to them, and allowing himself to be proselytized by the Reverend John Eliot, who translated the Bible into Algonquin. Passaconaway so liked the peripatetic preacher that he persuaded Eliot to live with the Abnakis. Eliot proceeded to convert the chief and his sons, including Wonalancet.

When Passaconaway finally gave way to Wonalancet in 1660, the old man delivered a valedictory (on which translators have

wrought havoc), which entreated his people to follow the way of peace. The Great Spirit had whispered to Passaconaway: "I have made them (the palefaces) plentier than the leaves of the forest, and still shall they *increase*! These meadows shall they turn with a plow—these forests shall fall by the axe—the palefaces shall live upon your hunting grounds, and make their villages on your fishing places! The Great Spirit says this, and it must be so! We are few and powerless before them! We must bend before the storm! The wind blows hard! The old oak trembles! Its branches are gone! Its sap is frozen! It bends! It falls! Peace, Peace, with the white man—is the command of the Great Spirit—and the wish—the last wish— of Passaconaway." The old chief retired to the long time tribal village in St. Francis, Quebec. Tradition has it that he died at age 120 and was borne to Agiochook in a sleigh drawn by wolves and carried heavenward in a chariot of fire.

The message of peace was not lost on Wonalancet, who was both a Christian and an aging man by the time he succeeded his father. But he found it nearly impossible to restrain his warriors from attacking colonists during the French and Indian War. Discouraged, he abdicated in 1685 and retired to St. Francis, succeeded by his nephew Kancamagus. As chief, Kancamagus tried in vain to control his increasingly belligerent confederation. Slighted by the colonial government, he finally acquiesced to the truculent factions of his tribe and eventually led them in raids on colonists. White settlers at Dover, a town near Portsmouth, took a brutal beating in 1689. But the bloodshed was not forgotten, and the settlers began a long retaliatory campaign, which ultimately rendered Kancamagus' victory pyrrhic.

The Pennacooks, Abnakis of the southern hills, were brought to their knees first, while northern Abnakis survived in the mountains. As the surviving Indians grew bolder and more vicious in their fighting, the government in Massachusetts responded by offering a bounty of one hundred pounds for every Indian scalp presented to the General Court, and by dispatching raiding parties to the North Country. Captain John Lovewell of Dunstable (later called Nashua) led several sorties, including one in February of 1725, that yielded his band one thousand pounds —ten scalps delivered to Boston. Lovewell had never bothered to ascertain whether his victims were friendly or hostile.

In April and May Lovewell returned to the wilderness, camping beside a pond near Pequaket. Lovewell had marched through one hundred miles of puckerbrush, a journey that had reduced his party to thirty-four men. They were awakened in the night by the sound of a gunshot. On investigation, the raiders found a lone Indian, apparently hunting. When they let go a few rounds, the Indian returned fire, wounding Lovewell and another colonist before dying in a fusillade. Meanwhile, Chief Paugus and his band of forty Abnaki warriors hid on the other side of the pond, where Lovewell's party had left its packs to pursue the lone Indian. After a quick count of the knapsacks, Paugus judged the odds to be slightly in his favor and shrewdly waited in ambush. When Lovewell returned with his men, the Indians opened fire. Both Lovewell and Paugus were killed in the skirmish, which continued under Ensign Seth Wyman and the warrior Wahwa. Finally, the Abnakis broke off and walked to nearby Pequaket, while Wyman's fit survivors retreated to Dunstable, leaving behind the seriously wounded.

SENSING the inevitability of white dominion, most of the Abnakis fled to St. Francis soon after Lovewell's battle. But some refused to be washed away by the white tide. Among those who remained was Chocorua, a prophet of the Pequakets. Despite the temper of the times, he was a peaceable Indian who befriended the local whites while maintaining his allegiance to his tribe. Legend says that, in order to spare his son the rigors of travel, Chocorua one day left the boy in the care of a white family, the Campbells, while he visited St. Francis. When Mrs. Campbell inadvertently left some fox poison unattended, the curious Indian boy sampled it. Chocorua returned to find a dead son and reasoned that white treachery, not accident, was at work.

The story of Chocorua's revenge is related in several poems, including one by Longfellow, but typical of the white view of the event is this excerpt from a narrative by Mrs. Lydia Maria Child, published in 1830: "From that moment jealousy and hatred took possession of Chocorua's soul. He never told his suspicions —he brooded over them in secret, to nourish the deadly revenge he contemplated against Cornelius Campbell.

"The story of Indian animosity is always the same. Cornelius left his hut for the fields one bright, balmy morning in June. Still a lover, though ten years a husband, his last look was turned toward his wife, answering her parting smile—his last action a kiss for each of his children. When he returned to dinner, they were dead—all dead! and their disfigured bodies too cruelly showed that an Indian's hand had done the work!"

Campbell led some friends in pursuit of the killer, and the group managed to run Chocorua onto a pinnacle jutting from the mountain that now bears his name. Campbell told the chief to jump to his death, but Chocorua replied that only the Great Spirit could command him to die. Campbell thought on this a moment and said, "Then hear the Great Spirit speak in the white man's thunder." Chocorua was staggered by the bullet, "but he recovered himself, and raising himself on his hands, he spoke in a loud voice that grew more terrific as its huskiness increased. 'A curse upon ye, white men! May the Great Spirit curse ye when he speaks in the clouds, and his words are fire! Chocorua had a son—and ye killed him while the sky looked bright. Lightning blast your crops! Wind and fire destroy your dwellings! The evil Spirit breathe death upon your cattle! Your graves lie in the war path of the Indian! Panthers howl and wolves over your bones! Chocorua goes to the Great Spirit—his curse stays with the white men!'"

No one knows how much of this story is true, but the legend has no doubt been embellished. A more plausible explanation of Chocorua's death is that, while wandering on his mountain, the prophet was discovered by a hunting party and killed for the going bounty of five hundred dollars per scalp.

By the mid-1700s most of the Abnakis had left their mountain homelands for St. Francis, but they continued to harass settlers on occasional forays for white scalps. So in 1759 General Jeffrey Amherst dispatched Major Robert Rogers and his Rangers to deliver the *coup de grace*. Under orders to destroy the village of St. Francis, Rogers and two hundred men left the fort at Crown Point on Lake Champlain and walked for twenty-one days through the wilderness. On reaching the perimeter of the village, Rogers and a couple of his officers disguised themselves as Indians and watched as the Abnakis held a great dance. Most of the tribe was asleep when the Rangers attacked before dawn. The rout was effective, in part because the raiders were shocked and incited by the sight of a few hundred of their countrymen's scalps dangling from poles in the village. Many warriors were killed, many others driven off as the Rangers plundered St. Francis and burned it to the ground. Among the treasures they stole from the church were a pair of gold candlesticks and a silver image. An old Indian, helplessly watching the theft, shouted at the looters, "The Great Spirit will scatter darkness upon the path of the pale-faces!"

AFTER the massacre Rogers' Rangers hastily fled south, staying together for about ten days until they reached Lake Memphremagog. With their food nearly gone, they broke into smaller parties, hoping to make hunting easier. The plan was to head for the upper Connecticut River and from there to go south through the western White Mountains to a town called Number Four, now Charlestown, in southern New Hampshire. Some made it, including Rogers himself, but others were overtaken by pursuing Indians, experts in the frontless warfare of the woods, and were killed or captured. A party of nine Rangers, the group

carrying the silver image, met an Indian runner, whom they pressed into service as a guide through the great pass of the White Mountains. A double agent, he dead-ended them in the high valley of the Sinoogawnock River, now Israel River, which falls from the northern Presidentials. Before leaving, he drew them a bogus map and poisoned their leader, the man carrying the silver image. Demented from the poison, he threw himself from a precipice and was buried in a cave along with the silver image. His comrades tried to find their way through the wilderness, but seven of them died in the pre-winter mountain storms. Only one member of the party survived. According to John Spaulding, author of *Historical Relics of the White Mountains* (1855), this "ragged and forlorn mortal had with him six knives, and in his bloody knapsack was a piece of human flesh, of which for the last eight days he declared he had eaten to support the flickering spark of life that now but faintly burned within him." Years later the skeletons of his comrades were discovered near the Sinoogawnock, and in 1816 a pair of gold candlesticks was found near Lake Memphremagog. The silver image, like the Abnaki culture itself, was forgotten.

Perhaps six hundred people of Abnaki descent now live about New England, with a small concentration at Odanak, the village —now a reservation—at St. Francis. Few traces remain of the Abnaki way of life. The scant information that survives about the Indian culture is found primarily in scattered collections of romanticized White Mountain history, written mostly by whites. One exception to this pattern is *Abnaki and English Dialogues*, published in 1884 by Chief Joseph. To write the book, a dictionary of the two languages, Chief Joseph had first to phoneticize the unwritten Abnaki tongue. His book, now out of print, is considered a major linguistic work. Joseph's son, Stephen Laurent, lives today in Intervale, New Hampshire, where he runs an Abnaki crafts shop and talks to inquiring historians about his forebears. One of Laurent's hopes is that someone will reprint his father's book, reviving at least a small part of the culture that has all but disappeared from the mountain region.

The conical lodges of the Abnakis are gone, as are their fish weirs and corn hills. Only a few burial mounds mark the passing of a people. The mounds are as much as sixty feet in circumference, and the Abnakis are interred in them face down along with their tomahawks and other relics. Nearby, scavengers have found earthenware pipes and kettles. Beyond these vestiges, only words survive today, and remembered events, all distilled by successive generations.

Even the words fail to capture the essence of the Abnaki culture, for the simple ways of this earthy, oral people are remembered, ironically, in the stiff, florid literature of the nineteenth century. "The Indian names and legends are shorn from the upper mountain region," wrote the Reverend Thomas Starr King in his book *The White Hills—Their Legends, Landscape and Poetry*, published in 1859. "They have not been caught for our literature. The valleys are almost as bare of them as the White Mountain cones are of verdure. What a pity it is that our great hills

> Piled to the clouds—our rivers overhung
> By forests which have known no other change
> For ages, than the budding and the fall
> Of leaves—our valleys lovelier than those
> Which old poets sang of—should but figure
> On the apocryphal chart of speculation
> As pastures, wood-lots, mill-sites, with the privileges
> Rights and appurtenances which make up
> A Yankee Paradise—unsung, unknown
> To a beautiful tradition; even their names
> Whose melody yet lingers like the last
> Vibration of the red man's requiem,
> Exchanged for syllables significant
> Of cotton mill and rail-car!

We can scarcely find a settler who can tell any story learned in childhood of Indian bravery, suffering, cruelty, or love."

AS THE Abnakis retreated to the North in the wake of Lovewell's battle, white settlers moved into the Saco River Valley. The Indian village of Pequaket became the town of Fryeburg, Maine. According to Benjamin Willey's *Incidents in White Mountain History* (1856), the land was granted in 1762 to a frontiersman, General Joseph Frye, on the condition that he "reserve one sixty-fourth of the township for the first Protestant minister, one sixty-fourth for a parsonage forever, one sixty-fourth for a school fund forever, and one sixty-fourth for Harvard College forever." The Indians were commemorated later, largely in mountain names. A peak near North Conway became Pequaket, the poetess Lucy Larcom gave Paugus' name to a mountain in the Sandwich Range, and the pond near Fryeburg where Lovewell was killed was named after him.

Villages too were named for Indian figures. The town of Chocorua stands on New Hampshire Route 16 a few miles north

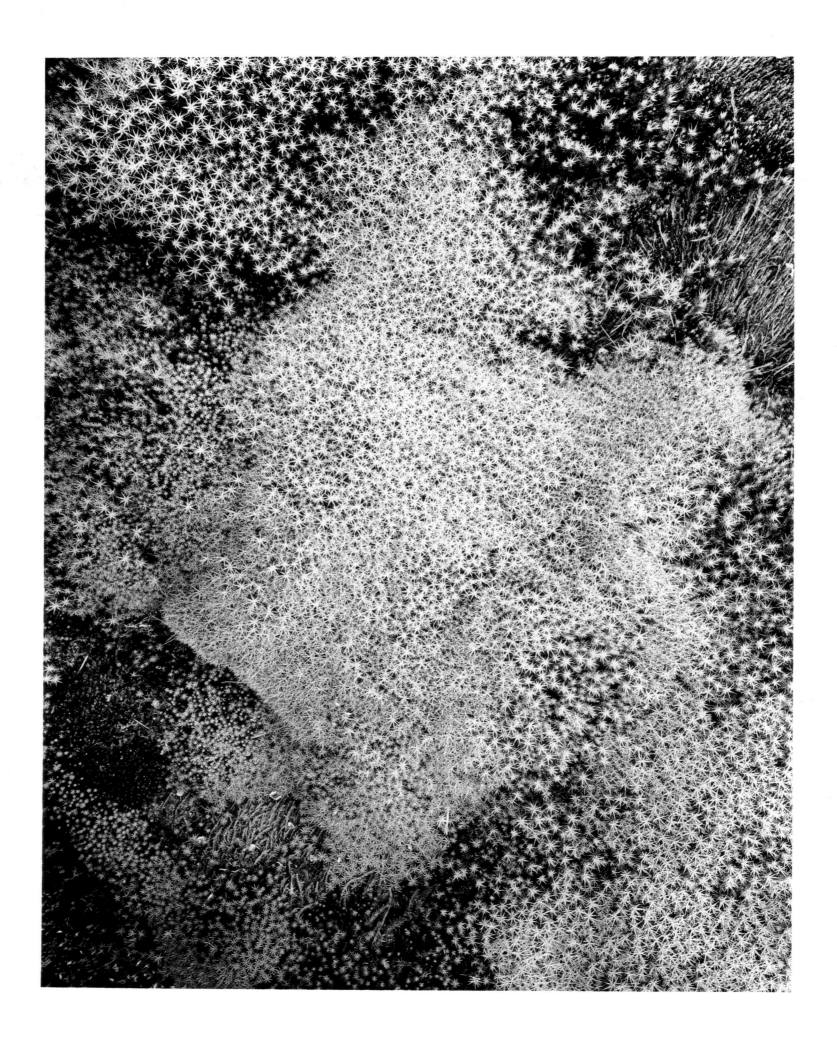

of the Indian Mound Shopping Center, quite near the peak on which the chieftain died. Cattle in the nearby community of Albany suffered a pestilence that for many years was believed to be the result of Chocorua's curse, until in 1821 a Professor Dana of Dartmouth College visited the town and traced the problem to a muriate of lime in the water supply. As Stearns Morse and John Anderson noted in *The Book of the White Mountains,* "Chocorua's curse at long last yielded to science, or one witchcraft to another."

High on a flank of Chocorua sits Camp Pennacook, a three-sided shelter for hikers. From there a stiff trail leads to the summits of Paugus, Passaconaway and Kancamagus. Well below the summits, the Kancamagus Highway runs east-west through the Swift River Intervale, where the Swift River Inn used to stand, and surmounts the height-of-land at a wangan ground—a place where Indians once gathered in celebration. A crisp, machine-routed Forest Service sign marks the wangan ground and the Kancamagus Pass, one of the many spines of the White Mountains. From the pass the road descends switchback on hairpin into the Pemigewasset Wilderness, named after the river that rises there and the Abnaki group that lived nearby. Until the 1950s, the Kancamagus was no more than two dead-end roads, pointing at each other over a broad stretch of mountain woods. Beginning in the late 1800s, a logging railroad ran on the western arm, and the eastern branch of the road serviced the town of Albany. Now connected, the Kancamagus Highway is a trans-mountain tourist road for people who prefer to take their wilderness from the back seat of a car. But thousands of hikers roam through here on foot, as the Abnakis used to.

North of the Pemigewasset the high peaks rise amid turn after concentric turn of lesser mountains. Agiochook looms in the center, massive, but probably not as large as it seemed when Darby Field and two unnamed Abnakis climbed it. The Indian name gave way to Washington when Phillip Carrigain's party climbed the peak in 1821 and whimsically affixed presidential surnames to the major summits of the range. The Great Spirit succumbed, nominally at least, to the democratic spirit. More recently it has succumbed to the commercial spirit as well. A clutch of buildings now stands on the summit: hotel, museum, weather sta-

tion, post office, snack bar, television tower and train station. A cog railroad ascends the west side of Washington, an automobile road the east side. A quarter million people visit the peak each year.

For all the development, there is still something untamed about Mt. Washington. The mountain sits at the confluence of several major storm paths, so weather is regularly dumped on it. And, like larger mountains across the world, Mt. Washington makes its own weather. The peak is boilerplated with ice for over half the year, and an average wind speed of thirty-five miles per hour prevails even in summertime. The highest wind speed ever recorded on earth was measured there in 1934: 231 miles per hour. Clouds swiftly form on one side of the peak and dissipate on the other, leaving it enshrouded much of the time. Snow falls on the summit during every month of the year. Hurricane winds blow on one day in three. Temperatures can go to forty-seven below zero, and the wind-chill factor has been known to drop as low as one hundred fifty degrees below. Mt. Washington, a 6288-foot mountain, has a treeline at 4500 feet—far lower than the 8000-foot treelines of taller but gentler mountains in the American West. In June, Mt. Washington's alpine zone is wild with mountain flowers, several varieties of which are common to Labrador and other northern latitudes. One flower, the dwarf cinquefoil (*Potentilla robbinsianna*) grows on Washington and nowhere else in the world.

The mountain is rarely free of storms, no matter what the season. Winds blast the southern Presidentials, pushing up over Abnaki Ravine. Storms on the northern peaks pass over the valley of the Sinoogawnock, where, according to legend, a poisoned ranger and a silver image were buried. They are fierce storms, and brief, their mad blinking too eery for human eyes, their electric roar too clangorous for human ears. It is said that long ago a hunter camping in the northern Presidentials was awakened during such a storm by a voice crying in the wilderness: "That pagan treasure from St. Francis must remain a secret to adventure till the Great Spirit's thunder dies in the crags of Agiochook." The words of a vanished people, issued by a mountain sky amid scattered darkness and the silver images of lightning.

The tops of mountains are among the unfinished parts of the globe, whither it is a slight insult to the gods to climb and pry into their secrets, and try their effect on our humanity. Only daring and insolent men, perchance, go there. Simple races, as savages, do not climb mountains, — their tops are sacred and mysterious tracts never visited by them.

—HENRY DAVID THOREAU

There are moments of stillness, plenty of them, when the autumn woods are yellow and red, misty moments and crystal clear moments of large calm. Let the wind rise, though, on a frosty morning when ice has glazed the backwaters of creeks even in wooded places, and all the world of the northern woods will run to a riot of red and yellow. Bright birch leaves are blown from the trees before their yellow gold has had a chance to brown. They fill the air by woodsides, they and the richer-hued leaves of maple, running the gamut of all reds from garnet to bright scarlet. The blood kindles on such a day. Prosaic folks even, dull fellows for the most part, plodders, stay-at-homes, "decent products of life's ironing out," feel the call to be abroad, to wander, to hunt, to know again the joy of muscles equal to unusual demands of their directing will. For the nonce the northern world of white men goes Indian in spirit as primitively as any Algonquin amuck on the trail.

It is the first week of October that knows, most years, the greatest glory of this countryside, the most wholesale display of Indian red and yellow. Then the lowlands are already come to their height of color, and dulling to tapestry hues; the lower slopes of the mountains of richest red and most golden yellow in maples and birches; and the middle slopes clear gold where the birches run up against "the dark woods," the serried ranks of spruce. Red and yellow, golden yellow, spruce-black, and granite gray, the mountains lift from foothills to bald peaks.

It is in late October or early November, after the leaves are down, that that so brief spell of good weather we call Indian summer comes to delight us. Then the kindly birds, the haunters of barn and dooryard are gone, the bluebirds and pewees and robins. There are sparrows about and many of the woodpecker tribes, but it is the screaming of jays and the cawing of crows that are loud over the countryside by day. By night you hear geese and a rare loon. From dawn to dusk the air is resonant, all the out-of-doors of stripped woods and pastures brown with bracken and lonely fields still green is like a great sounding board. The calm of Indian summer is not for long. The wind storms by and echoes and reechoes from all quarters. The days when deer are in season are at hand. Indian autumn we might well call this fortnight. Men are taking to the woods after the ways they have learned from the Indian. The spirit of the red man, reincarnated in the white, dominates a world reverting to the wild.

—CORNELIUS WEYGANDT

Skyline Promenades: I

MOUNTAINS! What stuff has been written in praise of them, what buncombe from dithyrambic pens! "As soon as men begin to write on nature," Emerson remarked, "they fall into euphuism." Ah, well: let no one be too full of blame or too stiff-necked in criticism. These lofty habitations of the gods, where they live and play and now and then look down amused upon the swarm of life in the valleys, are not to be re-created in pallid sentences, nor adequately understood by the minds of journeyman scribblers. Sometimes on wind-swept summits, if your ears are very sharp, you may hear strange conversations in an argot never known before, a sweeping language at a pitch inarticulate to common ears; a jargon, it must be, even to ears most sensitively tuned; yet full of some stupendous import. Those who listen best cannot translate it. The best are wanting here. Yet the day may come—who knows how soon?—when some chance super-listener may catch the meaning of it all, and "shake our disposition with thoughts beyond the reaches of our souls."

It would be illuminating to set down in an unimpassioned classification just what images and prejudices the word "mountain" brings to the minds of various people; in fine, to "dissociate the idea" in the manner of Remy de Gourmont. For in history mountains have meant various things, and even now they have no universal connotation. To earlier ages than this they brought all sorts of alarms; the Indians did not venture the higher summits lest they provoke the gods who lived there in awful seclusion. John de Bremble, who climbed to the top of the Great St. Bernard in 1188 warned his brethren against all such folly. "I have been on the Mount of Jove," he wrote, "on the one hand looking up to the heaven of the mountains, on the other shuddering at the hell of the valley, feeling myself so much nearer heaven that I was sure my prayer would be heard. 'Lord,' I said, 'restore me to my brethren, that I may tell them that they come not to this place of torment where the marble pavement of the stony ground is ice alone and you cannot set your foot safely.' There is every facility for a fall to certain death. Let us henceforth devote our pen to the narrative of more worthy matters." Less than a century later the mountains were still somewhat monstrous. King Peter III of Aragon, climbing to the summit of Rochemelon, found there a lake inhabited by monsters.

When the worthy monarch ventured to cast a stone into the water, "a horrible dragon appeared of enormous size which flew and darkened the air with its breath." But when Petrarch climbed Ventoux in 1335, he expanded and swelled after the fashion of moderns and moralized a little. And so, on this barren summit, he ushered in modernity.

But the mountains still stand for different things in the minds of different people: to natives they mean barriers; to lumber merchants, a far sweep of wealth; to tourists, a frolic; to climbers, a challenge; to revellers—boredom! To Pierre and me, who mask a bit of spleen under the purple robes of philosophy, they mean something more expansive, akin to composure. No doubt we ascribe virtues to them far too extravagantly and commit the "pathetic fallacy"; perhaps because we never go to them casually, but rather escape to them from the jangling city. To live for weeks in the tumble and confusion of the city; to look out of the windows on brick walls or smoky vistas; to use the fresh-fallen snow quickly churned into dirt and slush, heaped into brownish masses like a vile excrescence and finally sluiced down the sewers; to know that spring has come only by the gentle warmth of the air and tender buds on trees in the park, and then at length to be in the quiet and sweet majesty of the mountains is not to be scrupulously impartial. No: the change is too swift, too sudden and complete for academic thinking. The beauty is too overwhelming; the intellect is drowned in emotion. Philosophy does not prevail before that deluge of beauty. It is only before or afterwards that one may examine one's emotions and attach to them scientific labels.

Before or afterwards? And not that, either. If one cannot think clearly about the mountains in the face of their beauty, neither can one think clearly about them from the roof-tops of the city many miles away. For then one is romancing, building castles of air. O vain and strutting *poseurs!* Are the cities, then, all evil and the mountains all virtue? Or are we merely giving free rein to buoyant fancies?

Pierre and I give free rein to such fancies and, in truth, enjoy the sensation vastly. Sometimes we profess to be seeking the truth, to be plotting the road to Nirvana; but that is only our masquerade. Like most of our fellows, we, too, are discontented with things as they are, and indulge in that platitude which hangs

on every sophist's lips: that we are all the victims of civilization. We find the city distracting; we find the mountains by contrast to be places for general unburdening. There are those who sniff at our sentiments and find ragged holes in our reasoning. There are others, however, who for various miasmic reasons match our panegyrics with their own until the empyrean booms with verbosity. There are some few men of heroic self-confidence who have already deserted the city completely. But, pray, do not pin us down too relentlessly, or hold us by the beard of learning. We plead only for a chance to be ourselves, to feel soft earth at our feet, to see the broad expanse of the sky, to hear the wind in the spruce branches, to feel the warmth of the sun or the chill of the rain, to see valleys beneath us and peaks above, to bathe in icy pools in the silence of dark forests, to chop wood, hunt flowers, hear the birds, watch the clouds, eat, sleep and dream. For those who live in the city, the mountains have freshness and serenity, richness and flavour. Even the youngest of them are really mature. When Francis Parkman was lying ill in a rough camp on the prairie, he wrote: "I used to lie languid and dreamy before our tent and muse on the past and the future, and when most overcome with lassitude, my eyes turned always towards the distant Black Hills. There is a spirit of energy and vigour in mountains, and they impart it to all who approach their presence."

*   *   *

Pierre: Very pretty, very pretty, indeed. I suppose someone will be taken in by all that sentimental claptrap, but not I. Now, why do authors always have to weep before they get started? Why can't they begin—bing!—right at the beginning? This sort of moralizing is a weariness of the flesh. Come, stop pirouetting and get down to business.

The Author: Have patience, and we shall all get under way presently.

Pierre: Patience indeed, my good man. Let me have some matter as well.

*   *   *

Although some three hundred years of human planning and toil had gone into the making of Boston, and Pierre and I, too, had squandered most of our energy there, oiling the wheels and joints of the universe, it was amazing to see how casually we turned our faces away. Perhaps because we knew that two weeks hence we should return. Or perhaps because even at its best the city is no match for the country. At times that seems to be the truth. But what an insolent thought! If the vast sweep of wild mountain territory, virtually untouched by the "progress" of civilization, surpasses the complicated heap of the city for purposes of happiness, how abortive these achievements of mankind are! It was an old thought, smelling of philosophers no more recent than Socrates, but one, nevertheless, to be toyed with for a moment. It was not as though Boston were an ugly city. Some of those who make withering allusions to its past still recognize the unpretentious beauty of Beacon Hill, crowned by the gilded dome of the State house, mellowed by the informal sprawl of the Common, seasoned by rows of swell-fronted dwelling-houses— the whole agreeably redolent of unassuming life in homes. The cynics, the wags, the gay young criticasters to whom the world is an open book, concede that much to Boston. Yet two Boston-

ians, swelling with the New Englander's pride of place, rejoiced as they set out from the city.

We did not upset the decorum of the North Station. We did not provoke envy—nor derision. Boston at 6:30 of a Sunday morning was far too sleepy for such emotions, and beds were too recently lain in to be so completely forgotten. A few phlegmatic and sullen passengers with heavy luggage had stirred out this early for the only Sunday train to the White Mountains, and a few employees of the railroad were contemplating the day without enthusiasm. But they were all too much concerned with their own fortunes to bother about us. Indeed, the most active place we had found in the city was the Waldorf lunchroom in Causeway Street which we had entered an hour earlier with the clatter of hob-nailed boots and a banging of duffle-bags stuffed with camping equipment. Although at that hour, thanks to the forehandedness of a state daylight-saving law, the moon was still conspicuous while the sun was absent, and night still lingered over the city, the white-coated counterman poured our coffee from steaming urns and fetched dishes of ham and eggs from nowhere at all with an alacrity worthy of a week-day noon. In the arm-chair lunchrooms, night is only less brilliant day. Even though you visit them at that mysterious hour when the presses are pouring out the last editions of the morning newspapers, the coffee, the coffee-cakes and doughnuts, the bacon, the eggs, the ham and the hash are as wide awake as though they never slept. O marvel of alertness! As long as electric lights glitter all night on the enamelled walls of armchair lunchrooms, we need not despair of the world's business—nor its appetite.

If there had been any secret about our purpose, the packs would have given it quite away. For the equipment needed for a fortnight in the woods had risen impetuously above the drawstrings. After an hour or two of packing and repacking, Pierre, *le voyageur philosophique*, had compromised between decency and convenience by hanging the camp-ax outside his pack where it was exposed like a sinister warning to the curious gaze of all the world, while the lean handle of a frying-pan protruded from the top of my pack like the tongue of a collie gasping for air. That sort of thing passes well enough in the woods; but in the city it smacks of walking the streets unhatted; socially, if not legally, it is regarded as indecent exposure. "Going camping?" inquired a loquacious waiter who was polishing the white top of the table after we had finished breakfast. Our packs standing naked in the corner, we could scarcely dissent. "That's the way to spend a vacation," he went on dogmatically. "No use hanging around the city. Take it easy. I wish I could go myself. Hope you have good weather and a good time." With a look of real shame, Pierre then restored to the table two napkins he had just stolen for camp dish-cloths. Upon such casual words rest the destinies of empires.

There was no such welcome in the smoking-car of the mountain train. We turned over a seat for our duffle-bags and made ourselves comfortable for the long ride ahead. The half-dozen passengers in the car were scowling over their Sunday newspapers; the conductor frowned on us with a sanctimonious air which suggested that Monday would be more appropriate than Sunday for such a journey as ours. But we were sufficiently lighthearted to maintain a sort of social amiability even in so depress-

ing an atmosphere. After all, these men did not resent our presence; it was merely their Yankee manner.

After a day or two of drizzle and rain, the sun had come up warm and red, and was sparkling on the wet marsh grass in Revere and Lynn, and on puddles in the streets, as the train gathered speed out of Boston. We settled down dutifully to the voluminous Sunday newspapers, to their news as well as their galvanic feature articles—about a woman traveller who had brought back from Turkey the melancholy news that harems were going out of fashion; about the boot-and-shoe "magnate" who was building a "baronial castle" in the Ossipee Mountains —"Ill fares the land," the journalist implied; about other commonplace circumstances which in the newspapers assume the proportions of cataclysms. The news on the front page portrayed the case of striking miners and railroad men, and forecast a gloomy and bitter winter for all. Of such stuff is city life made. Bound for the mountains with a week's provisions in our packs, however, it was difficult to become excited. When you are lunching or dining in the city, it is well to maintain a vicarious interest in such matters. But when you are bound for the mountains, you are not disturbed because the millennium has not yet appeared. If the German Republic should fall before you get out of the woods, or the British Cabinet crumble—why, that would be worth knowing. Meanwhile, you have more pressing matters in hand.

After nearly five tedious hours of travel from Boston, through squalid cities and long miles of plain country, the train rolled across the Bearcamp Valley. We looked eagerly at the Sandwich Range as it came into view—Chocorua, Paugus, Passaconaway, Whiteface and, far away in the midsummer haze, Sandwich Dome, its eastern slopes torn with the ruin of fresh lumbering. The talk in the smoking-car had been boisterous and somewhat cheap. But as we rushed towards the mountains, conversation softened as though by an unspoken command, as though the very presence of the mountains rebuked pretentious chatter. As for Pierre and me, like sailors long out of port, we had seen land and were duly excited.

The sybaritic Henry Ryecroft, steeped for years in London, followed "an irresistible impulse" one spring to go into Devon. He was astonished at himself as soon as he arrived there. "Before I had time to reflect on the details of my undertaking, I found myself sitting in sunshine at a spot very near to where I now dwell—before me the green valley of the broadening Exe and the pine-clad ridge of Haldon. That was one of the moments of my life when I have tasted exquisite joy. . . . I had stepped into a new life. Between the man I had been and that which I now became there was a very notable difference. In a single day I had matured astonishingly; which means, no doubt, that I suddenly entered into conscious enjoyment of powers and sensibilities which had been developing unknown to me." As we clambered from the car at Madison and felt the quiver of hot hay-fields and caught the first whiff of the country odours—trees, hay, dust, flowers—we knew ourselves likewise to be different men; not better men necessarily, not more honourable socially, but at least different; and it is well to know as many phases of oneself as possible.

MADISON Station is four miles from the foot of Chocorua, where we planned to enter the woods. In the crowd which had swarmed to the station for the Sunday newspapers, there was one self-confident fellow with an auto "for hire." He lifted our duffle-bags into the auto while we took the rear seat. The little motor rattled over the rough country roads, bumped down the hills toward Chocorua Lake and clattered by the Pequaket post office to the foot of the Piper Trail. Above us rose the solid rock peak of Chocorua, on smooth ridges of green forest. We unloaded our baggage, adjusted our packs; and then, with a final look at the mountaintop, plunged into the woods, like Don Quixote on his first sally, "marvellous jocund and content," and with about an equal wit. From this moment our plans were somewhat undetermined. Our stores would last nearly a week without replenishment. Our spirits? Ah, there was the rub! Pierre carried a pocket microscope for examining plant blossoms. I carried opera glasses for hunting birds. *Pierre:* When we are fresh, we will lay out the day's work with your bird glasses. When we are tired, then, by Jupiter, we will use the microscope!

Although Chocorua (3,508 feet) is not one of the highest White Mountain summits, its beauty is the most haunting and the most memorable. On gentle slopes and ridges clad in beech, maple, birch and spruce, its summit of granite rises precipitously to a narrow tip, five hundred feet above the forests. From the south, across Chocorua Lake, this rocky peak cuts sharply into the sky—a challenge to all who climb. "Chocorua is not as big as the Matterhorn," writes Dr. Crothers, "but the principle is the same. It is every inch a mountain. And you have actually climbed Chocorua, while you only looked at the Matterhorn from the hotel." Especially in the winter, Chocorua does not suffer by such a comparison. Even from Mt. Washington on a clear day, the triangular cone of Mt. Chocorua is the most striking summit on the horizon, the one to which the eyes instinctively return. As we climbed on the Piper Trail and caught glimpses of the summit through the trees, we admired it, quite as the Zermatt visitor catches glimpses of the Matterhorn as he approaches that mountain valley and straightway forgets the surrounding peaks.

CHOCORUA.

They have the still North in their souls,
The hill-winds in their breath;
And the granite of New Hampshire
Is made part of them till death.
—RICHARD HOVEY

The most impressive outcrop of granite that I know is the cone of Chocorua. That cone is in sight from all the cleared parts of our farm, and it draws our eyes from our chores more often than any mountain about, though the bald cliff on Whiteface has a definite power of attraction, and the dark forests of Black, and the evening star over Israel. The horn, they call the cone of Chocorua hereabouts. Our neighbors note it as, sitting on our piazza, they catch sight of it from under the low arch that opens eastward. It is there, seemingly, just outside the barn door, when you look up from threshing beans. As you come in from the south field with a basket of astrachans, that horn of granite lifts before you, as it does when you are brushing, or hoeing, or picking stones.

Even though it is without snow from May to November, and unmistakably lower than many of its neighboring peaks, Chocorua is a true alp. It is bare, aloof, titanic, with a lonely beauty that at once softens and intensifies the sharp thrust to the heart its image always gives. All lights touch the granite desolation of its great cone with wonders of color, from the white flush of morning to the old rose of eve. It is an old, old mountain, the geologists tell us, older by far than its great neighbors of the Franconias and the Presidential Range to the northward. And age tells, too.

Granite ministers to us of New Hampshire living and dead. House on house has cellar walls of granite, and long slabs of granite under its sills. Granite doorsteps, so great we wonder how even oxen could haul them into place, are daily helps to its occupants so long as the house continues to shelter them, and they mark the site when, abandoned, it falls. A neighbor of ours who outlasted the house in which he was born had its door stone brought down to the churchyard where he wished to lie. On his death it was laid in the ground, its top level with the sod, and his name cut in it, making as lasting a memorial as man could devise.

There are men, New Hampshire born, who have used granite to preserve their names while they are still men alive. That instinct, which, in its baser form, leads to people scribbling their names in public places, leads also to the inscribing of names secretly in places far from where the world passes by. Forty years ago there came back to Bridgewater from the West one Cale Hunniwell. He wished to see the site of the house where he was born, to find again the apple tree from which he used to pick apples for his mother to make into pies, and to find where, in a pasture, in the moodiness of youth, he had cut his name on a bowlder. He was lucky. He found all he sought. The cellar hole was not filled up. The apple tree was still alive after fifty years, though it had been forced to grow upright to hold its own with the birches that had come up in the old orchard. There was a long search before the inscribed bowlder was discovered. In the end, his old chum, Tom, not Cale, put his fingers first into the lichen-filled letters. The bowlder was now in deep woods, for such the pasture had grown up to be in the half century since Cale had gone West. Cale scratched the letters clean again with a sharp stone he picked up. He had been sure he would find those letters. He knew they would still be where he had cut them. He had put his trust in granite, like a true New Hampshireman, and it had not failed him.

—CORNELIUS WEYGANDT

Outfit for an Excursion ca. 1850

The following will be a good outfit for one who wishes to make an excursion of days into the Maine woods in July, with a companion, and one Indian for the same purposes that I did.

Wear,—a check shirt, stout old shoes, thick socks, a neck ribbon, thick waistcoat, thick pants, old Kossuth hat, a linen sack.

Carry,—in an India-rubber knapsack, with a large flap, two shirts (check), one pair thick socks, one pair drawers, one flannel shirt, two pocket-handkerchiefs, a light India-rubber coat or a thick woollen one, two bosoms and collars to go and come with, one napkin, pins, needles, thread, one blanket, best gray, seven feet long.

Tent,—six by seven feet, and four feet high in middle, will do; veil and gloves and insect-wash, or, better, mosquito-bars to cover all at night; best pocket-map, and perhaps description of the route; compass; plant-book and red blotting-paper; paper and stamps, botany, small pocket spy-glass for birds, pocket microscope, tape-measure, insect-boxes.

Axe, full size if possible, jackknife, fish-lines, two only apiece, with a few hooks and corks ready, and with pork for bait in a packet, rigged; matches (some also in a small vial in the waistcoat pocket); soap, two pieces; large knife and iron spoon (for all); three or four old newspapers, much twine, and several rags for dishcloths; twenty feet of strong cord, four-quart tin pail for kettle, two tin dippers, three tin plates, a fry-pan.

Provisions.—Soft hardbread, twenty-eight pounds; pork, sixteen pounds; sugar, twelve pounds; one pound black tea or three pounds coffee, one box or a pint of salt, one quart Indian meal, to fry fish in; six lemons, good to correct the pork and warm water; perhaps two or three pounds of rice, for variety. You will probably get some berries, fish, etc., beside.

A gun is not worth the carriage, unless you go as hunters. The pork should be in an open keg, sawed to fit; the sugar, tea or coffee, meal, salt, etc., should be put in separate water-tight India-rubber bags, tied with a leather string; and all the provisions, and part of the rest of the baggage, put into two large India-rubber bags, which have been proved to be water-tight and durable. Expense of preceding outfit is twenty-four dollars.

An Indian may be hired for about one dollar and fifty cents per day, and perhaps fifty cents a week for his canoe (this depends on the demand). The canoe should be a strong and tight one. This expense will be nineteen dollars.

—HENRY DAVID THOREAU
The Maine Woods

At this point in the narrative of our journey, it might be well to consider our packs. As we plodded along the Piper Trail in the sultry noontide heat, we were considering them with remarkable frankness. Now and then the pungent spruce woods through which the path meandered rang with manly vituperation. The packs hung like lumps of lead; our shoulders ached and the sweat ran off our foreheads and arms and poured down our chests in tickling streams. O reader, perusing these pages in an upholstered easy-chair drawn close to the lamp: consider well your pack before you enter the woods. For automobiles and the lowlands have no greater reasons for being than the packs which hang on the backs of mountaineers.

At the North Station, Pierre had proposed that we weigh them. I protested that we could be no happier when we knew just how heavy they were. God knows our shoulders were balance enough; and if they ached, what matter whether the packs weighed twenty or one hundred pounds? The proof of the weight is the carrying. But being of that temperament which is not easily thwarted, Pierre drew the packs on the pan of the scales, and the full truth stared relentlessly from the dial: that mine weighed forty pounds while Pierre's weighed forty-four. We did not quarrel. On such matters Pierre is not disputatious, and fancies that though four pounds may be a physical burden, it is also a moral advantage. How unscrupulous one would be to tamper with moral balances! Yet, as we followed the mountain path, it was not noticeable that either of us complained the less, or sat down any the less reluctantly when rests seemed advisable. It is well enough to pick up your bed and walk, but the miracle becomes really a miracle when the kitchen and larder are added.

We had entered the forest at 10:45 (standard time). I had casually proposed that we climb the two miles and one-half to camp before luncheon, and cook our meal there leisurely. It is easy to make ambitious plans at the foot of a mountain. As the Piper Trail led us higher and the perspiration ran more freely, it was I again who breathlessly proposed that we cook luncheon beside Chocorua Brook, less than a mile from the foot of the trail. And the sun passed noon long before we heard that stream running noisily through a cool depression in the woods just as the steepest climbing begins.

To have lived in the woods, one must have cooked a meal over an open fire beside a noisy stream. That is as true as it is dogmatic. We crossed the brook gingerly from boulder to boulder and threw down our packs on a soft bank in the deep shade of the forest spruces. While Pierre drew out the frying-pan, mess-kits and provisions, I gathered an armful of dead wood and split up a small tree. We kindled the blaze against a rock, filled the coffee-pot at a pool in the brook, suspended it over the flames and filled the hot pan with sliced ham. Hence loathed melancholy! The forest no longer seems wild when the coffee-pot begins to steam and bubble and the frying-pan to sizzle. We had a meal of fried ham, pilot biscuits, coffee and fruit-cake—this last a token of maternal best wishes; and if our spirits had drooped a bit while we were learning the true weight of packs in hot weather, we now began to recover a sort of intellectual buoyancy.

At most a pound had been transposed from our packs to our stomachs. But there was still enough weight left, with a blanket each, an oilskin poncho, mess-kits, kettles, dry clothing, sweaters, and provisions of canned beans, rice, raisins, prunes, pancake flour, oatmeal, cocoa, coffee and pilot biscuits. For an hour or more we defied these bogies. We lay on our backs under the spruces beside the brook and blew puffs of tobacco-smoke into the air. And though our packs were not far away and silently admonished us for procrastinating, we insolently refilled our pipes more than once, while the talk flowed long and broad. There were two hours of physical exertion ahead of us—exertion such as no gentleman ever comes to know. But with the stream roaring close by and the sun dappling through the spruce-trees we were pleasantly oblivious of all that. And it was not long before we had agreed that life reduced to its lowest terms brought a wholesome satisfaction unknown to organized society. Agreement comes easily after dinner while the gourmands lie on their backs. How easy it is under favourable circumstances to reach brave conclusions about life, no matter how contrary the real facts may be! No sound business man forgets his cost of production and the closeness of competition when he talks with the directors through a haze of tobacco-smoke. Yet the man whose stomach is well filled can conjure the most glorious praises of life while his creditors are waiting just outside the door. After dinner, life dissolves her creditors or touches them with a magic wand which hurries them far away. But morning comes again, and the sorceries of dinner become once more artifices and pieces of play-acting. In business and in art the grey morn is disillusionment. But the surface philosopher of life knows no such disappointments. He may lose his temper in the morning; his spirits may sink quite low. But after dinner he will be once more contented and comfortable. He will thank God for his good fortune, and will rejoice that he is not as others are.

Soon after two o'clock we packed up once more, and by many spurts, followed by generous rests on the spruce needles, we reached camp by four o'clock. Camp Penacook is an open-faced log shelter, facing a huge natural fire-place, and commanding a long view down the mountain and over the country to the south and east—fields, hills, villages, Ossipee Lake, Silver Lake, Knowles and Whitton Ponds, and to the west a near view of the precipitous summit of Chocorua which rises five hundred feet above. Twelve hours earlier we had been clumping through the moonlit streets of Boston.

*　　　*　　　*

Pierre: Your account does well enough, I suppose, and is no less indifferent to the facts than any piece of literature. But don't ever forget that we suffered on that stretch from Chocorua Brook to Camp Penacook. It was torture. It was inhuman; by God, it was hell, and you might as well admit it. But, of course, I understand; we would have no literature if we always had the facts.

The Author: My dear fellow, facts are never more than fifty per cent of life. The rest are the things we don't understand and for which we go on living.

*　　　*　　　*

Our indolence and indulgence along the trail may have delayed our arrival, but at any rate we came into camp fresh. And as we examined this rough shelter, built and maintained by the Chocorua Mountain Club, our enthusiasm for the journey mounted. These mountain camps are too attractive in their combination of simplicity and sufficiency to be lived in for one night only. We set about distributing our stores along the slab shelves, laying out our blankets and ponchos and hanging up our towels and sweaters until Camp Penacook looked as though we were old inhabitants, or at least its owners. Behind the camp part way up the mountain was a dead spruce which had not yet fallen. We chopped it down, dragged it to camp, chopped it again into short lengths and split it into fire-wood. Long before we had finished supper and had washed the dishes, the sun went down behind the peak of Chocorua. Yet for a half-hour we could see it still shining in the valley, the outline of the mountain plotted there in a dark shadow, and could see a knob of the southern ridge still warmed when the valley was almost sunless. We ran down through the woods to the spring, dark and tranquil under the trees, washed the dirt and wood-smoke from our hands and faces, and performed a make-shift toilet, adequate under the circumstances though not altogether refined. It was the end of our first day—a day begun in the midst of the city and concluded in natural solitude, the whole bound by an exhausting physical struggle. We pulled on our sweaters as the air grew cooler, lighted our pipes again and stretched out at full length on the ledge before camp to watch the coming of the night—withal contented as animals.

A hermit-thrush, most reedlike of the White Mountain birds, sang again and again in a dark gully below. Mars came out red in the south-east. And as we smoked and dreamed, other stars appeared one by one. We counted seven, first beacons of the night. And fifteen minutes later we counted again; the total was fifty

when we resigned the task as impossible. Lights now began to appear in the dark valley, at Clement Inn and at Madison, and three others burned steadily far off on the shore of Ossipee Lake. Once we heard a brush on a ledge below; it was a brown rabbit leaping into a thicket. We were tired, but we were also contented and were loath to lose this scene in so useless a pastime as slumber. For a long time we gazed at the sky and at the dark peak above on the right where we hoped to be on the morrow. But at length the time did come for sleeping, and we undressed and wriggled into the sleeping-bags. Once during the night we were awakened by a stealthy noise too close by for composure. It was a porcupine, clumsy beast, investigating our store of provisions, some of which had not been put beyond his reach. We made noises ourselves no more civilized than his grunting, and he lumbered off in the moonlight. The other animals treated us with becoming respect; whatever they may have done they did discreetly. For even animals have civilized moments.

HOW THE White Mountains came by that presumptuous and misleading name no one seems to know. "White Mountains" implies summits so lofty as to bear perpetual snows. The occasional snow-squalls which flurry over the summit of Mt. Washington in the summer scarcely come within that category; and the snow-bank which lies in Tuckerman Ravine long after the June flowers have bloomed and faded vanishes as a rule before August is done. I confess that when I first visited these New Hampshire hills as a boy I was disappointed. Spurred on by the name "White Mountains," my imagination had sprung to ambitious conclusions which their height does not warrant.

We must not beat our breasts over the height of these mountains. What is the 6,000 feet of Mt. Washington to the 29,000 of Mt. Everest, the 20,000 of Mt. McKinley, the 15,000 of Mont Blanc, the 14,000 of the Matterhorn or Rainier? "Why, these are mere foot-hills!" exclaim tourists in New Hampshire to whom mountains mean the Rockies or Alps. Bless us! Of course they are foot-hills. Those who have stood on the summit of the Görnergrat above Zermatt and looked in awe at Monte Rosa, the Lyskamm, the sharp, defiant Matterhorn, the Weisshorn and other peaks far to the north, all sparkling with fresh-fallen snow, vast distances of white-capped, jagged peaks, snaky glaciers in every crevice, deep gorges, turbulent, foaming streams —whoever sees these peaks knows that *they* are the true "white" mountains.

We should do ourselves more credit and celebrate the beauties of our New England hills more effectively if we said less about their comprising "the Switzerland of America" and devoted our attention to their special characteristics—if, like Lord Bryce, we commended them for their friendliness, placidity and accessibility. To me also those are their chief virtues. The Alpine tourist responds to the sheer beauty of those lofty summits without always feeling the urge to stand on their highest rock. Most of those who do climb the Alps (unless they sneak their way to the top on funiculars) find it necessary to compromise their independence by engaging a guide who robs their pockets while he saps their resourcefulness. But the days are over when guides were necessary in the White Mountains, when Ethan Allen Crawford piloted adventurers through the woods to the summit ledges and finally up the cone of Mt. Washington. Now no one need fear going alone (except in uncertain weather), for the trails are broad, easy of grade and well marked. And so well mapped are these mountains that one has little to fear in rambling through the woods with no thought of trails. These are friendly mountains. One may *live* in them, while one is content to visit others, to look at them and to return at night to a comfortable hotel. "White" mountains, mountains topped with perpetual snow, excite adventurous propensities. Our New England hills, on the contrary, are tranquil. And they soothe. One has nothing to fear from knowing them.

This may not have been true one hundred years and more ago. When Darby Field made the first recorded ascent of Mt. Washington in 1642 the native Indians did not dare accompany him to the summit, for there the Great Spirit lived and no mortal could with impunity invade that divine domain. A certain awe of the mountains, which was less than fear and more than respect, coloured the writings of those explorers and adventurers who pushed into that region in the early part of the nineteenth century. Until the first road was built through Crawford Notch in 1774, most of the mountains in that vicinity had rarely felt the pressure of the white man's foot; and the mystery of what these woods and peaks sheltered, unduly stimulated the imaginations of travellers who looked at them from a distance. Travel along the Notch turnpike, built in 1803, soon became frequent. In lumbering coaches visitors came from the south of New England, and indeed from all parts of the world, spending the night in the old Crawford House, venturing up Mt. Washington, and in their diaries recording this climb which even now smacks pleasantly of novelty. The fatal disaster by avalanche at the Willey House in the summer of 1826 stirred the breasts of

If I must choose which I would elevate—
The people or the already lofty mountains,
I'd elevate the already lofty mountains.
The only fault I find with old New Hampshire
Is that her mountains aren't quite high enough.
I was not always so; I've come to be so.
                              —ROBERT FROST

mountain travellers for many years. Scarcely a traveller through the Notch road but dwelt on that subject in private or public letters, on the mighty forces of the mountain which when liberated may take human life; and the story of that great storm even now appeals to certain instincts in human nature. I never pass through the Notch without re-creating that avalanche in the mind's eye. But as the seasons have rolled on and the mountains have become more familiar, it is likely that those who go through or over them are no longer apprehensive of their wildness. The White Mountains are now almost as inoffensive as a city park. That has obvious advantages. But what a thrill they must have brought to travellers from the city in pioneering days a hundred years ago!

THOSE days, alas! are gone. Not adventure but conventional recreation now draws most of the visitors to this region. In a measure the White Mountains have been subdued; the lion has been tamed, and his tail may now be twisted with impunity. Railroads have made travel from town to town no more difficult than in the city; summer hotels with ball-rooms, golf-links and tennis-courts have softened and fattened life in the mountains; broad, graded paths have made climbing in the Presidentials no more difficult than Sunday afternoon climbing in the Palisades; the proud summit of Mt. Washington was first roped by a carriage and then thrown by a cog-railway, and defiled by the architectural excrescences which those who pander to summer tourists "run up" quickly; hard, oiled roads through the places of wildest beauty serve merely as speedways for neurotic automobilists whose first thought when they descend at night concerns their mileage. The mountains are now infested in places by those dull persons who spend the autumn "in town," the winter at Palm Beach and the summer recuperating on the summer-hotel porch. As unimaginative society has moved in, the expansiveness and freedom of the White Mountains has been squeezed and limited. Much still remains, however, for the pedestrian who is more enchanted by deep ravines and secluded waterfalls than by the appointments of his hotel and the variety of its cuisine. Boott Spur, Tuckerman Ravine, Great Gulf, Carrigain, Whiteface, Passaconaway, Paugus—these have not been smirched by the egg-eating tourist. But the "childish fear" experienced by Thomas Cole when he first beheld the features of the Old Man in Franconia Notch in 1828, and the thrill which Francis Parkman felt when he visited the mountains in 1841—these are not often duplicated now.

Yet the independence and strength of the mountains is by no means dead. Some of those climbers who have set out above the tree-line of Mt. Washington in defiance of unfavourable elements have paid with their lives. A monument, a wooden cross stuck into a pile of rocks, a memorial tablet or two, serve as grim reminders of those tragedies. The scrub growth existing in rock crevices above the tree-line, torn, snapped and pounded by gales of fabulous strength, sometimes of more than 175 miles velocity, the summit rocks blackened, chipped year by year by occasional temperatures of 50° below zero, broken and cracked by frost, these bleak, barren, desolate, forbidding summits above the tree-line, these "unfinished parts of the globe," bear witness that the

mountain still can snarl. In some measure, I, too, have tried the mettle of the mountain's temper. For once in August with a party of boys I was caught in a summer tempest at the Lake of Clouds Hut at the base of the Mt. Washington cone. On the day before we had walked cautiously across the peaks from the Madison Spring Huts in opaque clouds which sometimes made objects a few feet away invisible, dampened the rocks until they dripped, and blew through our clothing until we were numb. During the night the wind came up; rain, hail and snow rattled against the heavy glass windows of the hut. All the next day the storm beat against the hut, whistling, roaring, shrieking, buffeting the door so that once open it could be shut again only with difficulty, stinging the faces and hands of those who ventured outside until they were glad to seek shelter again. After another night the storm somewhat abated and we ventured out, and at length walked into the shelter behind Mt. Pleasant, and down into the warm sunshine of the valley where the weather had been fine all the while. Those hardy fellows of fifty years ago who maintained a U.S. Weather Station on the summit of Mt. Washington all winter, while the icy blizzards rocked the little structure which sheltered them, blew the carpet off the floor, and kept the temperature below freezing three feet from the red-hot stove—they knew the stuff of the mountains. The tourists who on fine days ignominiously climb Mt. Washington by the cog-railway can scarcely realize what diabolical strength lurks in this wilderness of mountains and valleys which on every side stretches placidly in the summer sunshine.

In the gratuitous task of taming the mountains the lumbermen have had far too large a share. Their sharp claws, scratching nearly every slope in that region, have torn away the flesh. Once when the first settlers were pushing their way north and in the day when Abel Crawford moved twelve miles south into the wilderness of Hart's Location ("rather than to be crowded by neighbours," as he said protestingly), white pine, hemlock and spruce flourished all through the White Mountains. In those extravagant days no settler's cabin was too humble for its white-pine frame and spruce finish. Pioneers chopped down the virgin trees and burned them in huge piles to clear the land. Lumber had little value in the commerce of the early White Mountain settlements. During the last century the state of New Hampshire sold its holdings ridiculously cheap, and most of the lumber companies have hacked their way into the forest ruthlessly. The real wilderness of the White Mountains, what is tritely known as "the forest primeval, the murmuring pines and the hemlocks," has practically vanished. Far too few now are the lots where virgin spruce-trees rise a hundred feet in the air, branchless for half their length, straight, true and sound, in whose tops the wind blows all day like the wind which twists the weather vanes atop the church steeples. It is a rare delight to walk through such woods as still remain: woods where the undergrowth of birch, poplar and maple is almost absent, where the floor of the forest is soft and clean, and the sound of the wind majestic and sonorous—with no suspicion of the cacophonous babbling of the wind in hardwoods. One day such forests stretched through all the mountain vales; and he was indeed a vain man who could walk through them without paying spiritual tribute to their mysterious Maker.

In view of the toll which various whims and passions of society have exacted from the White Mountains it is amazing to know how much beauty still remains for those who wish to see it. Backroads pedestrians may follow grass-grown ruts high up in the mountains to some abandoned farm-house. There the mountain towers abruptly on one side, and on the other the valley stretches for miles over hay-fields and wood-lots to other hills almost lost in the haze and quivering heat. On the Davis Path from Bemis to the summit of Mt. Washington, campers may climb steadily for nearly three days on the Montalban Ridge, camping at night in open-faced shelters, all the while in deep woods. There are streams which tumble from springs and pools well up under the mountain peaks; their little secrets of waterfall and gorge are kept for persons who scramble along the mossy banks or climb from boulder to boulder in the river bed. And no matter how unscrupulously the lumber "kings" have ravished their domains, the contours of the mountains still remain—the smooth bow of Moosilauke, the sharp peak of Lafayette, the burly bulk of Carrigain, the jagged teeth of Tripyramid. And from every summit the variety of colours, rhythms, forms, cloud effects, green intervals, gleaming lakes, has resisted the inroads of man. New England has nothing else so beautiful to offer. Who can say how much good it has done to New Englanders, or how far the effect of its serenity and friendliness has travelled in an impatient world?

*　　　　*　　　　*

Pierre: There, now certainly you must be done with preamble! Surely, my friend, literature or no literature, it is time to begin the story.

The Author: Look here, old man, a little of this amateur criticism goes a long way. The trouble with you is that you have no feeling for art, and you don't realize the importance of orienting the reader so that his mind meets yours directly. You can't stop a strange man on Fifth Avenue and begin: "We left Boston on Sunday morning at 6:30." He would simply think you were mad, and I for one could not contradict him. If you are going to

write you must lead the reader on smoothly and gently, cajoling, urging, guiding and all that sort of business. In fact, you might say that the reader, being an inferior—

Pierre: Just so, just so. Let's begin right here.

*　　　　*　　　　*

An hour before we were up on Monday morning we lay in our blankets, heads bolstered up on the duffle-bags, watching the mist in the valley and the sun growing warm on the peak, and listening, too, for bird-voices. Day comes quietly in the mountains, with none of the initial bustle of the city. But there are virtues, withal, in this acceleration of the city day, for in a measure it prepares one for living. We squirmed out of our blankets towards seven o'clock to what at first sight was an inhospitable world. Where now were the fires and steaming coffee-pots on which to begin the day? The world was no longer concerned with our presence; that came as a bit of a shock. But not long afterward the camp-fire was snapping, the oatmeal pot was rattling merrily, the coffee-pot was sending out a long banner of steam, and pancakes were smoking in the frying-pan. And so we recovered our poise and congratulated ourselves on a certain rare genius for adaptability and an underlying strength of character. There was no one near by to gainsay us.

Bird-songs were indifferent and sluggish with the advance of the summer. We listened in vain for the white-throated sparrow who a month earlier had been the most brilliant singer in the mountains. While breakfast was cooking, a purple finch faced the warm sun and sang as feelingly as though he, too, expanded with the breath of a mountain morning. And in the dark woods around the spring where we washed the sleep from our eyes and bodies, chickadees and kinglets made merry. Somewhere down the mountain a winter wren "uncorked his song" and ran on beautifully through trills and runs and warbles—an expression not of ecstasy but of deep and pleasant content.

After breakfast was cleared away we packed our duffle-bags carefully; and when that chore was done we set them outside the shelter where we could not see them—these ogres of camping life

—and dawdled about camp, smoking and dreaming. Ah, but they were heavy packs! Pierre insisted that we ought never to be in a hurry, and if the burden of progress compromised the profit of our promenade—why, then, let us make no progress at all. Surely Camp Penacook was pleasant enough for a prolonged visit. There was virtue in what the man said.

From Camp Penacook the tip of Chocorua rises five or six hundred feet above a fringe of woods and a final temple of bald granite. We thumbed the map, and speculated on how far we might reasonably journey before nightfall. It looked easy enough on the contour-map. We might cross Paugus that day, with a little determination, and climb to the top of Passaconaway. Or Camp Shag on the crest of Paugus might prove far enough. It all depended on what good or bad fortune the day held in store. Well, we decided to take a fling at climbing, at least to the top of Chocorua; and at length we struggled under our packs. Great God of Russia, what a trail! In the woods we gasped and staggered, clutched at the trees for assistance in climbing, and rested at frequent intervals. The serenity of morning in the mountains became now purely an academic point of view. Up above the tree-line, when the goal was ever in sight and each foot of progress shortened the distance perceptibly, we climbed more contentedly. But the morning was well gone before we stood on the top of the mountain

The view was hazy. The rugged mass of Paugus, the pyramid of Passaconaway, even the long swell of Whiteface, were distinct enough, but the mountains to the far north were painted out of the picture. Carrigain and its graphic notch were barely visible and at times entirely obliterated. For sometimes at that precise point where the haze destroys visibility, a gentle breeze is enough to suggest faintly and then quite to blot out a distant line of mountains. We were not the first to climb Chocorua, despite the fact that we had slept so near the summit. Already a young woman had tubes of paint spread out on the summit and was painting this midsummer view, while her comrades sat round her listlessly. We discussed the view—conventionally, sentimentally and artistically. The painter remarked that hazy weather in the mountains is after all the most beautiful, for it stimulates the imagination. It does. And how much more vividly a clear day enlivens the fancy! That sort of prismatic weather reveals a vast scenic wealth, and it also paints in mental images the fabulous wealth which lies just beyond the horizon and all through the universe, wealth to which human eyes are necessarily blind and human ears deaf. We are not endowed with natural beauty so parsimoniously that all that is visible on a clear day exhausts our coffers. Even though we travel through all the world on the wings of the wind, a lifetime is too short and human powers are too weak to respond to its infinite variety.

If parents desire to expand the minds of their children beyond the wires of the city-cage, let them look at, and become familiar with the woods, the wilds, and the mountains. Let them not trust to the conventional formulas of poets and novelists for just ideas of nature. Let them receive early impressions from nature herself, and then the descriptions of writers will be fully understood and appreciated. Then we shall no longer hear grown people express a wonderment of what is natural; nor see enlightened men bring art as the standard by which to measure nature, instead of judging art by nature, the mother of all art.

—NATHAN HALE

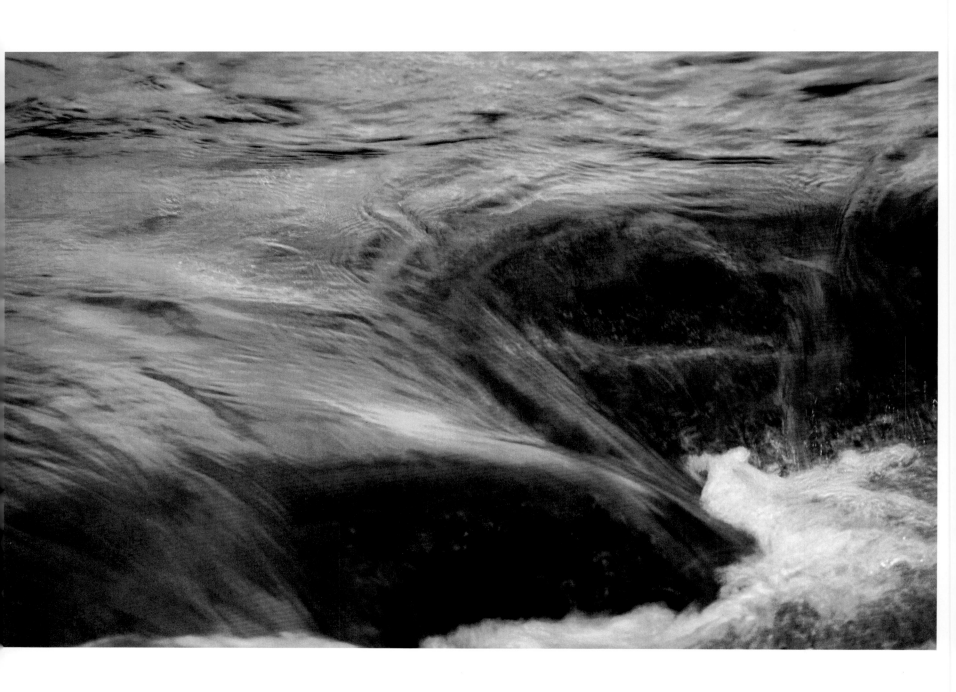

II

IF the proposal to go on that day to Passaconaway had been entertained seriously, even at the moment when it was made, we soon forgot it as we loitered on the summit of Chocorua. The sun was hot; the air, lifeless. We spread out the map, counted the contour-lines which fell away from Chocorua to Swift River and then rose swiftly up Paugus, consumed our morning ration of chocolate, and talked with the others who had climbed the mountain. A party of climbers from the south advised us as to trails and expressed genuine interest in the project of our journey. The prospect of a week or two in the woods, dependent only upon an occasional store for replacing the stock of provisions, fires the imagination of those who like to climb. We fancied that these people envied us, even while they were unwilling to shoulder such heavy packs. You do not try the mettle of mountains from the porch of a hotel or boarding-house. No, you must take "pot luck" with the woods and the weather. From the cool veranda and the comfortable hammock, mountains are deceptive hoydens. "He who knows what sweets and virtues are in the ground, the waters, the plants, the heavens, and how to come at these enchantments, is the rich and royal man."

Now, it was apparent to these sympathetic people that ours was a pleasure trip, and it was necessary for us to play our part accordingly. What is more ridiculous than a man who makes a chore of recreation? It was necessary, therefore, to put on a brave showing, at least as long as we were in sight. We shouldered the packs again, buoyantly as though they were nothing in particular, made our adieux hurriedly before the sweat began to run too profusely, and started down the peak carefully, making sure of each step, in the general direction of Paugus. The people on Chocorua summit watched us until a twist in the trail cut off the view. When we were certain of this we pocketed our pride and sat down under an overhanging ledge. The low, rambling summit of Paugus (3,248 feet) seemed almost contemptuously insignificant from the vantage-point of three hundred feet higher,

but we regarded it with well-calculated respect. Our way lay down the western ledges of Chocorua, through a burned patch of forest on the "Bee-Line" Path. The sun blazed hotter every minute, and the air was far from invigorating. And the task of descending carefully, making due allowance for the pushing force of the packs, and trying each footstep before entrusting ourselves to it—all this was a nervous as well as physical strain. We rested without shame; we wasted time imprudently. We lingered over a tiny stream of water which was the one cool spot in this dry, dusty, burned area. It was nearly two o'clock before we reached Swift River for a legitimate pause in the day's journey.

Swift River is a broad mountain stream rushing through a stony path between Chocorua and Paugus. We found a deep, oval pool in it near the junction of the "Bee-Line" Path with the Bolles Trail, the trees leaning over it on every side. In a few minutes we had a fire of driftwood snapping at the edge, the coffee-pot swinging close to the flames; and while the water was heating we undressed and plunged into the river. Mountains have no surer tonic than these cold streams which gather their water from the summits and carry it through the shade of evergreen forests. But no one bathes in such water; plunge and retreat —that is the formula. And so we plunged, soaped ourselves thoroughly, and then plunged again until we felt clean and refreshed. We hung our sweaty clothing in the sun, and in the garb of tropical savages we cooked our luncheon and ate it. It was cool and comfortable sitting on the rocks, sung to by a noisy stream whose voice, heard in such close proximity, is never dull —a succession of mezzo-soprano notes against a background of wood-wind instruments, a perpetual "Unfinished Symphony." It was there, as the hands of the watch passed three o'clock, that we officially abandoned Passaconaway as a goal beyond the bounds of pleasure promenaders. Paugus rose at our backs, a grim reminder of hard work still to be done before nightfall.

IN these woods and mountains we were not concerned with details; on the contrary we were concerned with masses and generalities—with the peaks of the mountains rather than with the innumerable twists of the paths up which we scrambled, with the sweep of the woods rather than with the individual trees, with ranges of hills, horizons, shadows, clouds, the flood of sunshine.

And that was in a way the contrast between life in the mountains and life in the city. Whatever refreshment we enjoyed sprang from this sudden freedom from the tyranny of details and that exhausting confusion of innumerable petty affairs which puts a high premium upon city living. An Olympian might live serenely in the city and see nothing but a black mass of people in the streets and a long jumble of high buildings, some soaring above the others, as the aeronaut looks down upon Manhattan from an altitude of 2,000 feet. What he sees, however, and what develops in the photographs he snaps, is not the city—but the shell of the city. The city is the people, the procession of individuals busy about their individual affairs, the people on the streets, all through the office buildings; in the tenements, apartments and dwellings; in theatres and concerthalls and galleries —the people everywhere who have made the physical city and for whom the physical city exists. One knows nothing of the city and misses its fascination who knows nothing of who these people are and how they live—in sum, who knows nothing of the details. The details exhaust those most intimately concerned, but they are nevertheless the city's life-blood.

Most of us city-dwellers lead fairly active lives and come directly in contact with many people, indirectly with many more. The details of this small traffic would overwhelm us if most of them did not automatically fall into certain categories where they look out for themselves. But we have only to stray a bit outside the routine of our existences, walk to the office by a different route, go to a new restaurant for dinner, venture into an unfamiliar corner of the city, or meet a new man in another business or another social circle, to learn not only how little we know of this human life close by, but also how feeble our understanding is of that which passes immediately under our eyes. No use crying in despair that we can never know a millionth part of this one city. The point is, we are not alert.

Manhattan is a microcosm of peculiar beauty, with its noises, colours, vistas, far-flung buildings, the pageantry of crowds, and stories written on strange faces, the sunlight and the shadows, the river "maculated with craft," as Huneker phrased it, such stuff as Balzac saw in Paris, Dickens in London, and Juvenal in ancient Rome. Yet if this opulence offends the delicate eye and seems merely tawdry, one can always relieve it by gazing at the sky, at the same sky which enfolds the country. Especially if one walks at evening by the river, agleam with the myriad-lighted ferry-boats and tugs, they stir the imagination. Sometimes on crisp winter evenings I see the Great Dipper flickering above the buildings at the south end of Washington Square. For the city boasts its own magic and necromancy, especially in the evening, with the glow of window-lights, street-lights and heaven-lights all blending, all related parts of the universe.

Now and then I like to be alone in the city and to walk with the tide of traffic. Especially on Saturday afternoons in the springtime, Fifth Avenue streams with holiday promenaders—a stream dammed at times at cross-streets until the corners are choked and running over; then released by the traffic signals it is swallowed up in the main current which flows the full length of the Avenue. These are smart people, for the most part, smartly dressed, walking with an air of composure. And they *are* composed, too, at least amid this company, even the vast majority of them who privately struggle for a living and blunder through the succession of private disasters which punctuates human lives. Here at least all reflect the splendour of this one avenue where the riches of the world are gathered and arrayed enticingly in shop-windows. It is an amiable throng, privately oppressed, paying tribute every hour to the growing complexity of civilized life; but it is in no mood for revolution. Changes in economic life are reflected here as quickly as the changes in modes and manners; but the changes well up from other springs. This is a throng decidedly contented, minding its own affairs as no other throng in the country, but with mutual neighbourly interest nevertheless. This is the most tolerant mart in America. For here the thirty-dollar clerk rubs elbows with the millionaire and thinks nothing in particular about it. Even in Washington Square where foreigners quite outnumber the native Americans, and the children of foreign parents roller-skate and "stump the leader" so energetically that walking becomes a peril—even here, a stone's throw from squalid tenements and exotic tearooms and intellectual garrets, one looks in vain for an anarchist. Anarchism —social, literary or artistic—may simmer and seethe in the neighbourhood garrets or among the serious thinkers of the near-by clubs, but not in the Square on springtime afternoons or evenings. Those who are walking there or lounging on the hard benches may have mordant thoughts about the social system, but they are too languid, too content as animals to bother about serious matters.

But the city is not all detail and gregariousness. Even in the midst of the maelstrom a secluded nook or two provide shelter. Indeed, sometimes I fancy that the solitude we make for ourselves in the very centre of the city is the more enchanting because it is deliberate; whilst the solitude of the woods cannot be remedied. At any rate, I like to push through the Saturday afternoon crowds on Fifth Avenue, past the snobbish lions sniffing the air before the Public Library, past the fashionable shops, past the Waldorf-Astoria with self-conscious luncheon parties at the windows, past the silk-stores with iridescent, blazing strips of fine stuff in the windows betokening a softer, richer civilization than ours—past all this and then a few steps along a side-street and up four flights in a musty apartment-house to the rear lodgings where I live. This house is doubtless the least desirable in the street, somewhat decayed, lost amid higher and cleaner buildings, badly ventilated, dark in the hallways, and inhabited by a fly-by-night sort of company into whose business one dare not inquire too earnestly. A commercial artist of pleasant manner and real aspirations lives on the same floor. I know none of the others, not even the couple who live in the next rooms, whom I hear coming and going, but whom I have never seen. The others pursue their own affairs in their own unobtrusive way, and by their attitude suggest that the less known the better.

There are seven windows in my apartment, all with human prospects. One faces a neighbouring apartment inhabited by a kindly, white-haired woman whom I see reading the newspaper every morning. We are separated by two walls and a space of ten feet, but we have never spoken or nodded or shown the slightest neighbourly feeling. The other windows look upon dingier subjects—a rear alley, a jumble of grimy brick walls, ugly fire-escapes, electric wires; but above the western wall looms the top of a Fifth Avenue building where I can see the sun in the morning before it has passed over the brick summits above my apartment.

Here are none of the stately dignities of gentlemen of the Old World, none of the fragrant formalities of living, none of the goings and comings of seedy scholars with hollow eyes or gay young wastrels with flaming cheeks. On the contrary, here are worked out the destinies of a hundred laundresses, seamstresses, tailors and dealers in silks, who may frolic a bit after six o'clock if they are not too weary from nine hours of labour, but who have little to amuse them during the day. This is no place for spacious living. For spacious living is not a product of machine civilization and self-imposed materialism.

But in such places as this we create solitude in the city and free ourselves of details as thoroughly as by going to the woods. The rumble of traffic never ceases, even during the night; in foggy weather the tug-boats screech mysteriously in the North and East Rivers; fire-apparatus screams down Madison and Fifth Avenues several times a day, a weird, uncanny, shrill, terrifying rush and tumble, a true urban fanfaronade. Thus the pulse of the city is always throbbing on our ears. There is solitude here nevertheless, as refreshing as that of the woods; and a solitude quite free of loneliness. In places so constantly concerned with the means of living it is well to reserve corners for contemplating the ends—even though they be no more tangible than fays and sprites. For perhaps, like Jean Paul, we who dream

amid our own books and papers, pried upon by nothing more animate than the wall-clock, may wake and find that nothing has gone but our sleep. Our daytime occupations after all are no more progressive than a sort of martial "beating time," keeping the machinery oiled and fed so that time may not be lost. We cannot look beyond the farthest whirling gears. For more distant and opalescent prospects we must cultivate places for solitude and loneliness.

THOSE who climb Paugus, less euphoniously known as Old Shag or Toadback, are by no means numerous or altogether wise. The lowest of the Sandwich Range, with no single peak commanding a broad view, it is also one of the most difficult to ascend. For everywhere the slopes are steep, and they culminate in a succession of cliffs which are inaccessible save in a few places. And since the lumberman has carried away the huge trees on the south and east slopes, a quarrelsome growth of maple and birch makes the woods fairly uninteresting. A stubborn mountain, reluctant to be conquered, it kept us scrambling, puffing and sweating until half past six. Soon after we were fairly started on our climb a hermit thrush flew into the thicket. I "squeaked." He came nearer through the leafy second growth cautiously, by short advances alternated with anxious moments of peering under the leaves, until he was nearly over our heads. Only when birds are so near that their markings can be seen with the naked eye do they seem clean and precise of pattern. This quality of their plumage does not appear in stuffed specimens in glass cases, "museum-coloured." Indeed, birds lose so much of their individuality in death, their attitudes and personal characteristics are so significant, that stuffed specimens are not always immediately recognizable. Near the last ridge of the cliffs we saw a young junco, but lately from the nest, his white tail-feathers exposed like starched skirts. He did not closely resemble his sleek parents, had none of their smooth slate-grey, and if he had not chirped quite in the voice of his parents we should scarcely have known him.

But we were neither bored nor exhausted as we climbed Paugus this stifling afternoon. On the contrary, we conserved our strength, and lest the periods of conservation be set down as blank spaces in our lives, as vacuums (which *human* nature does not necessarily abhor), we laughed and joked, discussed and speculated, "tossed and gored," all in the boisterous, resonant voices for which the woods are well suited. And to lend a touch of regularity to these volatile moments we adopted a system of "official" and "semi-official" rests. The body governed both number and length of semi-official rests. When our legs ached, our breath came in short gasps, and our hearts throbbed almost noisily, semi-official rests alone made further progress possible. And although he who was in the rear sometimes complained of the length of a spurt up the mountain, neither complained of the number of these brief pauses. Far less gross and by the same sign far more ethereal were the official rests. The soul governed them and the spirit indeed flourished upon them. For they came to be rests of twenty or thirty minutes when we took off our packs, sprawled on our backs, lighted our pipes, drank at a spring when that was possible, and talked at large about the world. How

many tremendous thoughts are lost because no reporter is present? How many scintillant jests for the same reason waste their fragrance on the desert air? How many bold ideas, apophthegms, even plots for novels and lines of fragile verse have you lost for ever, dear reader, because they flew through your mind just before you fell asleep? Such thoughts came in bewildering abundance at every official rest. They rustled for an instant in the spruce-trees. The birds heard them, and, astonished at their profundity, took flight and were seen no more.

It was after six when we climbed the last steep place in the trail, surmounted the last cliff, and came to the easier, rocky grade where the trail twists over the ledges three-quarters of a mile to camp. A sense of luxury at being so near the end of the day's march made the last stretch a long one. We were for ever resting, indulging ourselves, and we took a sudden interest in the history of the trees which grew in this difficult exposure. Their entire competence for this life seemed a reflection upon human beings who struggled under them. It had been a wearisome day, a sore trial on unaccustomed muscles, but a sense of expectancy now kept us going. The trail wound through the trees mysteriously; each turn in it promised to be the last. And finally we came to Camp Shag, built in a sort of summit plateau, a deep spring a few steps behind it. Before supper was finished the night had fallen black under these tall spruces, many of which were a foot thick through the butt. We washed our kettles by candle-light and dried our sweaty clothing before the fire while we sat comfortably with our backs against a tree. Through the black branches the stars flickered silently. And although we were tired we still put off as long as possible the business of drowning the quiet majesty of night in sleep. Every moment was really too precious. There may have been porcupines near us that night, or even bears in that mountain fastness, but we slept too soundly to hear them. And the sun was well above the horizon before we were astir the next morning.

*   *   *

Pierre: Well, I see that, after all, literature has its limitations. What interests me most about your piece is what you leave out rather than what you put in.

The Author: Art, my friend, is selection.

Pierre: Life, old inkpot, is one damned thing after another. Literature is too blamed snobbish to admit that. Now, what you don't get in your precious scribbling here is the sense of physical exhilaration in this day's climbing. You curse out the packs and call on the reader to shed tears over our hardships and paint us as martyrs of a sort, which is all good literature in good literary taste and tradition. But while we were scrambling breathlessly up Paugus there was also a physical exultation, a close contact of physical body against physical obstacle, every muscle pulling hard—a contest from which we emerged as the victors. I suppose that is too vulgar for literature. Art goes on the theory that arms and legs are to be looked at but never used. Well, it is

not even quite safe to ogle them. All I can say is I'm glad you weren't translating your thoughts into art that Monday afternoon on Paugus. Otherwise I should never have managed to pull you up to the top of Paugus as easily as I did. Go on, now; let's become literary again and get over the ground as quickly as possible.

*   *   *

There was real work to be done on Tuesday, through some of the wildest and most refreshing country in the White Mountains; and we were eager to get under way. More scientific mountaineers than we might have approached the work more wisely, however, and might easily have got under way a full two hours before we did. But what's to be gained, save an hour or two in the evening; and why should men carry into the mountains the efficiency they devote to city business? Well, we never did that in the mountains, except once when the circumstances compelled it. We lingered over breakfast, packed the duffles leisurely; and when everything was in readiness for the march we made a peace offering to the gods, smoked one pipe all through without hurrying, and let the essence of Nature, the essence of the trees and sunshine and the birds and the far sweep of sky, seep through our consciousness before we got under way.

From the summit of Paugus, where at nine o'clock the sun was pouring down pitilessly, we looked at the black spruce-clad tip of Passaconaway and at the rugged country which lies between— the steep western slopes of Paugus, a maze of forest and granite cliffs, the ungainly hump of Hedgehog and an unnamed mound which rises towards Passaconaway. It was not difficult to remember that once the red-skins hunted in such forests, and under the successive rules of Passaconaway and Wonalancet waged war against other tribes and the invading white man. By ten o'clock we were descending Paugus on the Lawrence Trail, over ridges bristling with stunted trees, down steep gravel banks formed by the crumble of the ledges where the granite rocks have been split by the frost and washed by the rain. Down we went steeply and then along the side of high, wooded cliffs, taking each footstep cautiously lest the weight of our packs upset us and send us tumbling in the forest below. We crossed the face of the monstrous Overhang where the view up and down a serrated ridge is equally stupendous. If we had scant footing as we pushed through this country, the trees had hardly more. For every inch of girth and altitude they had worked untiringly. They grew from crevices in the cliffs and between heavy boulders which they had gradually thrust aside. And their roots, enjoying the ease of no rich depth of soil, ran all over the mountainside, interweaving and intertwining, until the floor of the forest had become a bewildering tangle. Whence comes their nourishment? They must be sturdy trees to flourish in such country, like the first settlers who cleared the fields on the mountains a century and more ago.

We decided to climb Passaconaway by the Walden Trail which ascends the steep slope of Hedgehog and then dives and leaps over another ridge to the cone of the mountain. The guide-book made no mention of water on that side of the mountain. In weather which kept so much water on the exterior of our bodies we had no desire to parch the interior, for neither nature nor the human disposition thrives on such an inequality. Below the Overhang we came to a spring bubbling joyously at the base of two huge maple-trees. Pierre cried: "Official rest!"—dropped his pack and dipped his face into the spring, while I was close on his heels. Having filled our cups more than once we sat down with a tree as luxurious back-rest to enjoy the sublimity of a hard-growth forest and to console ourselves for the work ahead by congratulating ourselves on the work behind. The woods were songless and silent, except for a vague whirring like the machinery of a distant sawmill or of a distant automobile engine. As we consumed our ration of chocolate, sipped the cool water and smoked our pipes, the sound came several times. It was a partridge drumming near some fallen log a few rods off in the forest.

Fearing drought for the rest of the day, Pierre filled his canteen as we left the spring, and it was fortunate that he did. For the woods through which we climbed all afternoon, well up towards the tip of Passaconaway, were hot and waterless. At noon we were in the wild valley between Paugus and Passaconaway, where we began the arduous ascent of Mt. Hedgehog. Why this hump is so contemptuously named (especially since another mountain five miles north bears the same name), we did not know. But surely the posterior of the ubiquitous hedgehog, when his quills lie pointing to the rear, is no more angular and is no more forbidding when seen from behind. We climbed the back by brief, determined marches which left us breathless and sweaty, but always nearer the top, and then we walked across the top of the ridge in search of water. Alas! there was none—not even the Ancient Mariner's teasing plenty. It was nearly two o'clock when we abandoned the quest and prepared our luncheon of baked beans over a fire built on a rock in the midst of the woods. But the beans, nutritious as the label ungrammatically proclaimed, did not quench our thirst, or stimulate our enjoyment of this bit of old forest. We laid hands on the canteen, pressed its damp covering against our cheeks and cooled our parched throats with frugal gulps. The dishes and frying-pan were soiled, but water was too precious for so vulgar a use as washing. We cleaned them quite as effectively with branches of leaves. It is said that raspberry leaves clean dishes as thoroughly as soap and water; only a middle-class prejudice kept us from resorting to that method throughout the entire journey.

*　　　　　*　　　　　*

Pierre: Why do intelligent men climb mountains?

The Author: I doubt whether intelligent men do.

Pierre: Yet surely you would not dissent if by some strange chance you were described as intelligent.

The Author: No, indeed. I should consider that description conservative.

Pierre: Do we climb mountains because they symbolize life—because the grade is always up and they fret the way with minor details?

The Author: Nonsense, old fellow! Life is not like that. I defy you to prove that it is constantly mounting higher, or that its obstacles are minor. If life were as arduous as the rump of Passaconaway we should all remain indolently in the valley. No: life pays best in proportion to your content and lack of personal ambition, your unwillingness to rush on to the summit. Really, old fellow, how naïve you are!

Pierre: Naïve, am I? Well, at any rate I don't talk merely for effect, for vain show, and especially in company I'm not likely to impress. But to return to our muttons, mountain-climbing is something in the nature of an achievement. That's what attracts the climbing throng. Otherwise they would be quite as content to walk through level woods.

The Author: That is largely true. And we also climb mountains because they carry us into a new world. Thoreau said somewhere in his Ktaadn essay that mountain tops are untamed parts of the universe whither it is a slight insult to the gods to climb and pry into their secrets and try their effects on our humanity. No patch of level woods has the wealth of exotic impressions which you may get on mountain summits where the wind blows as it never blows on level ground, and where the trees fight for existence as they never fight down below, and where the birds and flowers and nearly everything else have individual qualities.

Pierre: Hold tight, old boy! Don't get breathless over words. There is plenty of climbing still ahead.

*　　　　　*　　　　　*

We slipped the mess-kits into the packs again and started on towards Passaconaway. We descended sharply in a ravine between two clumsy humps and so lost much of the altitude we had won at the cost of throbbing hearts. Then up again, hands, knees and feet, grasping at convenient trees for support, pulling up one almost precipitous rise where our stomachs were close against the cliff and our feet were none too secure. And then over a minor summit where the trail vanished in a tangle of blow-downs, and from which the cone of Passaconaway loomed up pleasantly near at hand. As if inspired by a diabolical will to dampen our spirits, the trail now deserted the logical route across a level col and slipped far down the eastern slope, setting us the gratuitous task of regaining this altitude by a steep and sandy gully. We might curse and threaten, but we were as helpless as middle-class society; and as Pierre remarked, you must climb mountains on your feet, and all your piety and wit cannot cancel half a yard. When we were half-way up the gully we did mock the devil temporarily by declaring an official rest and plucking raspberries which had ripened in the sun. But the mountain summit above us did not shrink while we loitered. Despite the disappointments, the thirst and discouraging nature of the climb, however, the most difficult part of our day was over. At the head of the gully a trail pointed directly towards the setting sun. We followed it on the precipitous mountain side, through woods where tough bunches of roots were as intertwined as the Laocoön, to a spring of ice-cold water singing to itself in the wilderness. And a half-hour later we climbed to the camp, at an elevation of 3,600 feet.

We had seen no one since leaving Chocorua on Monday noon. But now as we approached camp we found it already occupied

by two lads who were cooking the last of their supper. Their greeting was as cordial as though we were old acquaintances. They had been at work for the past month on the trails leading up Paugus, Passaconaway and Whiteface, and had improved all the paths save the Walden Path over which we had come that afternoon.

We set about splitting wood at once; and as night crept down over the mountain and the only light came from the dancing flames, we finished supper and laid out our beds. Then all four sat down close to the fire and compared notes—not merely of the woods, but of those larger subjects of life with which all mortals concern themselves. Such meetings are explorations, intellectual adventures, in search of common ground. And what joy it is to discover behind strange features and strange voices the old landmarks of comradeship. It was not merely that these new friends liked to sleep and cook in the open and loved the trees and mountains where they worked all day. Beyond all this they, too, were concerned with life, were eager to know what was false and what true, were on the watch for beauty and kept the windows of their look-outs clean lest something of value escape them. They had their fields for observation, as we had ours, for no man can watch the entire landscape. But for all that the principles are constant, and it is rare to find two whose fields have not overlapped. And so by the time our fire-wood was gone and the flames had become spasmodic, we all knew roughly what property we had in common and what each held in his own right. It is the virtue of intellectual property that all may profit by what one holds alone, and no matter what demands are made upon it the owner is none the poorer.

In three days we had accomplished what moderately vigorous walkers might do in two. We made our ambulatory renegation one hundred per cent instead of fifty by declaring Wednesday a prolonged official rest. We were none of your scientific men who weigh their packs carefully, plan their schedule and hang to it day in and day out. Our packs, albeit heavy, were sufficiently well-provided with food to sustain us three or four days longer.

So we made a super-holiday of this fourth day in a fortnight of holidays; on the fourth day we rested from all our works and kept it holy.

Those who are hunting birds destroy their chances of seeing many when they hang to a fixed schedule. Birds warm to idlers better than to the important people who bustle along the road and trail with a preoccupied expression on their faces. We had a substantial breakfast that morning, what with oatmeal, griddle-cakes, bacon, crackers fried in the fat, and coffee. But the birds singing in the tree tops, swinging in the sunshine, and calling to one another in clear tones drew us away from our meal more than once. Most of them were birds with which we were familiar, either by plumage or song. The chickadees, kinglets, juncos, blackpoll warblers and Canadian nuthatches we knew, without being any the less interested in them. But the others, whose volatile songs rang out in clear tones, brought us to the opera glasses and at times led us a quiet chase around camp. They were purple finches and American crossbills, common enough to mountain tops in New England; but the crossbills particularly, who made nothing of flying close over our heads, were to us something in the nature of a novelty. So keyed up were we to the chances of seeing rare birds that when a hairy woodpecker started drumming fifty feet up on a dead tree we were determined to make him out one of the less common three-toed woodpeckers. Fortunately he remained some time in one place, leisurely spreading out one wing and then the other, giving us ample opportunity to identify him by the book. Being in search of the truth, no matter at what cost to human vanity, we abandoned the quest for three-toed woodpeckers. In amateur ornithology the will to believe ranks high. When birds are so numerous and elusive as they are in New England, and can be identified positively only by tiny markings, the ambitious amateur with more enthusiasm than judgment has no difficulty in compiling impressive lists of rare birds seen in the most unlikely places. For although he is not sure that he has seen a Bohemian waxwing, neither is he sure that he has not. When the amateur returns

There are spots in the mountains which are marked for resting-places. No sign is there saying this. It is like a tacit, long-standing agreement of all those who, by plain or devious ways, emerge here from the solitude and will soon have vanished into it again. . . . Every resting-place has put itself into shape somewhat in order to please and attract, even though there be only the merest indication of possible comfort.

Over the spot, however secluded it may be, there lies a gentle breath of sociability. A great, invisible, common bond embraces and unites all the dwelling-places of human society, and it is as if a thin thread reached up here into these most forgotten corners of the high mountains. Someone has already been here, perhaps only yesterday, and someone may yet come, from anywhere.

—Julius Kugy

with less remarkable bird lists, his honour as well as his knowledge of birds has improved. In human affairs the will to believe makes for little good.

As the morning advanced and we considered our various businesses and household duties for the day, it was evident that we had no time to waste. We had clothes to wash, fire-wood to chop, a dish of prunes to stew, a book to dip into, an afternoon's walk to Whiteface; whilst I was charged with the responsibility of keeping a vigilant eye on the birds, and Pierre made hourly observations of the sun with the compass; and both of us had myriad, confining responsibilities towards the clouds, the haze, the wind and the views. But lest noon be on us before we had commenced the round of duties we descended at once to the spring rippling through the moss and needles a few feet below camp. Here we washed ourselves and then washed our soiled clothing. Like Roman slaves, the birds immodestly pursued us to the baths. We hung our wet clothes on a line in the sun (where they made a tranquil, homelike appearance) and put on the dry ones we had brought in our packs. It was already late for stewing prunes.

Amid the kettles and provisions in our packs we had a book—to supply the wisdom of a third party if perchance our own should rub bare. And lest the imported wisdom should prove inferior to the native (for which we had unconscionable respect), we had chosen our book most deliberately. Our choice fell on the discourses of Socrates by Xenophon and Plato, in one of those translations happily prepared against charlatans who cannot read the original. A happy choice! While lunch was cooking we read aloud Socrates' "Apology," before the verdict, after the verdict and before the sentence, and after the sentence of death. It went as well as, nay, better, in a rough log shelter near the summit of Passaconaway, than in the heavily charged atmosphere of Academe. For up there we were less concerned with the reasoning than with the man whose trial of his own case rippled with sardonic gibes and dry humours even while his life was at stake. We laughed at the points over which Socrates no doubt chuckled to himself; but I think we were both moved when after the verdict he turned to his friends in the assembly and said calmly: "There is no reason why we should not talk together while we can, and tell each other our dreams. . . . When I left home in the morning, the signal of God was not against me, nor when I came up here into the court, nor in my speech, whatever

I was about to say; and yet at other times it has often stopped me in the very middle of what I was saying; but never once in this matter has it opposed me in any word or deed. What do I suppose to be the reason? I will tell you. This that has befallen me is surely good, and it cannot possibly be that we are right in our opinion, those of us who hold that death is an evil. A great proof of this has come to me; it cannot but be that the well-known signal would have stopped me, unless what I was going to meet was good."

*   *   *

The Author: By Jove, he was a *man!*

Pierre: Truly he was. Of course, his argument in defence of himself could hardly have pleased the court and put it into a sober mood of impartiality. The defendant owes some duty towards the jury. If they are to return a just verdict he must not call up their personal prejudices by deliberately antagonizing them.

The Author: Yes, that is true. And it also shows Socrates to have been a most virtuous man, or he could not have been so indifferent to his fate. When it comes to a matter of life and death most of us are too distracted for dreaming.

*   *   *

It was delightful to be in camp (quite as delightful as being on the march), to be fixed, with the fire burning all day, the clothes swinging on the line, the lodge furnished with our belongings, with our provisions in one corner, our blankets airing in the sun, our two books within arm-reach (the bird book and the fountain of wisdom), the map to tell stories of unknown country, the compass to fix our place in the world and our relation to it. For all things are relative, and for sentimental humans the mountains boast half their charm by contrast; and our enjoyment of the woods was largely that we had brought our home into them. We sat in the doorway, languid in the sunlight, occasionally getting up to mend the fire and to watch the progress of the stewing prunes. That was business enough—keeping the heat constant, moving the kettle to one side when the liquid boiled too furiously, pouring in fresh water, laying on a new stick of wood, kicking the embers into a glowing heap. It was truly life in close contact with the essential elements which compose it.

Whiteface summit lies two miles to the west by a path on the edge of a mountain bowl. It was three o'clock before our duties

LOOKING DOWN

Dear World, on the peak we miss something,—
    the sweet multitudinous sound
Of leaves in the forest a-flutter, of rivulets
    lisping around;
The smell of wild pastures in blossom, of fresh
    earth upturned by the plough;—
But the fields and woods led us hither; half-way
    they are following now.

One world—there is no separation—the same
    earth above and below;
Up here is the river's cloud-cradle, down
    there is its fullness and flow.
My voice joins the voice of your millions who
    upward in weariness grope,
And the hills bear the burden to heaven,—
    humanity's anguish and hope!
            —LUCY LARCOM

were done, and by that time thunder was rolling ominously in the north-west. We put everything under cover, including a supply of fire-wood, and then started swiftly on our way, hoping to reach Whiteface before the storm broke. To the left of the trail was the precipitous cirque between Whiteface and Passaconaway, so deep that the bottom was faint in the haze. We were only half-way to Whiteface when rain began to spatter. The centre of the storm was to the east, but the edge of it moved overhead, black with clouds, scud and rain, and booming with long rolls of thunder. The beauty of the storm was magnificent. In the north the sun disputed with the clouds, setting gold off against the black. In the south the Ossipee Mountains were a study in blues as the storm swept over them—deep blue to the east, on Shaw and Blacksnout, turning gradually to blackish blue on the west where rain was falling and the clouds were heavy. Eager to see the entire panorama, we set out rapidly, through the wet forest and before the rain was quite finished, for the summit of Whiteface. When a second shower sprinkled large drops of cold rain on Whiteface we ran into Camp Heermance, where our two friends who had been working on the trail were waiting for the storm to pass over. While it roared outside we sat chatting and smoking inside the camp, entertained by two juncos which flew in and out without fear. Finally the black clouds blew away, leaving the north-west a mass of pure gold. The wind blew up fresh and very cold. We returned to Passaconaway, cooked supper in the gathering dusk, and sat up until the fire expired.

IN THE WHITE MOUNTAINS

Mountains in whose vast shadows live great names,
On whose firm pillars rest mysterious dawns,
And sunsets that redream the apocalypse;
A world of billowing green that, veil on veil,
Turns a blue mist and melts in lucent skies;
A silent world, save for slow waves of wind,
Or sudden, hollow clamor of huge rocks
Beaten by valleyed waters manifold;—
Airs that to breathe is life and joyousness;
Days dying into music; nights whose stars
Shine near, and large, and lustrous; these, O these,
These are for memory to life's ending hour.

—RICHARD WATSON GILDER

CONWAY MEADOWS.

FROM the summit of a mountain the city seems incredibly remote. The rolling expanse of yellow fields from which the hay has just been cut, miles of smooth woodland, occasional gleaming lakes and ponds, and other mountain peaks which cut jagged outlines or expand smoothly into the horizon, shut out thoughts of the distant city. Only fellows with supple imaginations can realize that while they are sitting in the shelter of a summit ledge and looking meditatively over this untamed landscape, this last stronghold of the natural wild, clumsy motor trucks are lumbering over the city streets, factory chimneys are fouling the air with soot, newspaper presses are vomiting the latest tittle-tattle, and city pavements are so filled with preoccupied pedestrians that the more impatient of them are hurrying along the edge of the streets. It is hard to recognize in the luminous blue of the sky above the mountains that torn, grimy fragment which now and then contemplative men see between the rows of tall buildings in the city. For the city and the mountains have little in common.

What with gossip, politics and business, the eddy of city life spins fast. Those who are caught in it never touch the ground until at last they are planted unresisting in it when life goes out of them. By competition they live; competition finally kills them. Years of dull work which they frankly deplore and which draws hard lines in their faces sometimes yields them a place in which to live. Behind them, on either side of them, and often above and below them, they are squeezed by other walls and floors where others are also existing. But there is no ease in such possession; the toil must not be relaxed. Those who have bought their homes must needs work as hard to keep them. For others who also live by competition are digging a little here, tunnelling a little there, and woe be to the property-owner who does not set an alert watch day and night lest his home be undermined. The city streets are lined only with the fruits of competition; only competitors are admitted. No wonder that the Christian virtues die, and that they might be forgotten entirely but for the presence of costly churches built on the fruits of competition, many of them mortgaged like the houses in which the parishioners live. Faith and charity are soon strangled; hope alone remains.

The most deadly poison which city life distills is the vanity, pomp and artificial importance it ascribes to itself. Caught for life in the vicious circle of competition, working day after day not to improve the man but to keep body and soul together, the city-dweller concludes that this manner of life is important. Nay, he considers it the most important in the world. He has heard of the universe in only a vague way. Let him talk to the astronomers who find this planet infested, not graced, with human life—to whom the problem of human life is only a silly tangle. From childhood to old age he is saturated in the city's material wealth. The value of its land in dollars and cents is stupendous. The size of its buildings and their number baffle the imagination. Its streets are filled with endless streams of expensive automobiles. Through miles of underground ways the subway trains rush at incredible speed, carrying an incredible number of passengers. Those who live in such an atmosphere are soon fascinated by the brilliance of its procession. They have no natural contrasts, no unsubdued mountain peaks, nothing of permanence, of reality, to sober the sophisticated struggle.

Yet those who have penetrated beyond the outskirts of civilization know how many vices she carries in her train. Lewis and Clark found the Indians of the Far West honest, dependable and friendly; but the Indians who had come in contact with the white traders stole their horses when the explorers did not watch closely. Anthropologists to-day do not find the Kwakiutl Indians of Canada invigorated by their contacts with the white man's civilization, and Stefansson finds the Eskimos beyond the Arctic Circle weakened and rendered profoundly unhappy by the busy-body teachings of the white missionaries. The Sunday newspapers and popular magazine advertisements which picture the distresses of "three o'clock fatigue" and offer a panacea of "setting-up exercises," the melancholy of the clerk who gazes longingly at the glass door marked "President" but is reduced to the slavery of the time-clock, and the confusion of the untutored chap who clumsily drops a spoon in an élite restaurant and does not know what to do about it—such advertisements suggest that even for the civilized, civilization comes at high cost.

But many of us weary of words at times and look beyond ideas for the fundamental satisfactions of life. In the clangorous city we find many of them, but alas, at what a price! May we then turn to the country or to the tranquil villages of the country and rest our minds while we ease the pain to ears and eyes? It is difficult to make a clear decision. The country and the town breed certain satisfactions; they fall somewhat short, however, of Paradise.

Some weary dwellers in the city, with a romantic turn of mind and the common superstition that good is merely *not bad*, that virtues are merely *not vices*, and that morality is all that is *not immoral*, fly hopefully to the country. For a few brief weeks in the summer they have escaped the tumult of the city and have found peace in the natural serenity of the country, the eternal stability of the mountains, the strength of the forests, the busy assurance of forest streams which pour down from the summits. They expand spiritually in the quiet of broad stretches of countryside and respond likewise to the sweet odours of newly-ploughed land or fresh hay. At night they see, perhaps for the first time, the huge expanse of sky; and in the number and the brilliance of the stars they find closer kinship than they ever knew before. They feel at last that they *belong*, that they are part of the great universe. Day after day the sun bakes the hayfields, but these citizens on a promenade do not wilt under it as they do on the hard city pavements. Sometimes for a week at a time the clouds hide the mountain peaks and "vex the vales with raining" until the streams threaten to undermine the rickety road-bridges. But they do not tire of this spectacle as they soon grow weary of continued rains in the city. "Nature is an excellent sedative," said Chekhov, who lived in a more stifling intellectual period than America ever knew. "It pacifies—that is, it makes one indifferent, and it is essential in this world to be indifferent. Only those who are indifferent are able to see things clearly, to be just and to work. Of course, I am only speaking of intelligent people of fine natures; the empty and selfish are indifferent enough anyway."

Amid the friendly mountains of New England there is an end to the din, the fury, the welter of competition, which characterize city life; and despite the fact that dollar democracy has sent its advance agents to the White Hills and the lumber pirates have hacked their way through most of the forests, leaving desolation and slash in their inglorious train, the mountain scenery seems no less serene. It is still a very real element, very substantial, most stimulating; and for men whose eyes are sensitive to delicate touches of beauty, it never wants variety. "Nature is a mutable cloud, which is always, and never the same," said Emerson. In the summer, haze, rain and sunshine afford a ceaseless variety. In the autumn it glows day by day with a new beauty. In the winter the higher summits covered with hoarfrost glitter brilliantly in the sunshine. And in the late spring the variety of sensuous greens climbing the mountains and crowned with the dark tones of the spruce-trees is truly astonishing. For the amateur the variety of birds and flowers provides an endless quest.

Of course, nature is by no means perfect; the tornadoes, the heavy wind-storms, and the extravagant methods of seed-distribution suggest that. But it is never so mediocre as large masses of humanity. And man does not improve it. Formal gardens, carefully laid-out parkways, public gardens, scientific plantations of trees, disciplined, cultivated, tamed—all these miss the essential beauty of the broad sweep of the out-of-doors. They are as emasculate as matinée idols. Only braggadocios fancy they can contribute substantially to nature from their own pompous personalities. So the outdoor painters like Corot, who copied nature with fidelity, surpass in their art the classical landscapes of Claude and of Turner, who believed that no landscape could be painted without human figures.

COMPETITION has robbed the city of natural beauties and the spiritual values which accrue from them. In their place, however, in the very midst of the pushing and shoving, the city has nourished other very real beauties whose values are surely as great. It is in the city that Shakespeare and Molière are played, the Beethoven symphonies heard, the Van Dycks, the Millets, the Rembrandts hung. Rubbing elbows with the hurrying throng of competitors is that buoyant world of aspiring artists, aglow with the hope of accomplishment. There, too, are craftsmen who take joy in doing their work well; business men who by faith keep commerce from being sordid; social workers who have the good of their fellows at heart; and thousands of inconspicuous citizens who are not distressed by the sour smells of their environment and who light-heartedly keep themselves sweet. It is a gay life and a cool life in the heat of the city. It is a life, moreover, attendant upon sublime satisfaction, which keeps them looking out rather than in, which increases their range of perception.

From the summit of a mountain the city seems incredibly remote, but the art and beauty which live in the city and even flourish on the spoils of competition seem close at hand. These

human accomplishments are not lost in the majestic sweep of mountains and valleys. The same exaltations, the same spiritual rhythms, spring abstractly from natural and human beauties. Strange that so fragile a flower should blossom in the coarseness of the inchoate masses of the city, as the lily flourishes in the black slime of a swamp. But sufficient that it does live there. And sufficient that citizens who keep themselves attuned to it are balanced by it and so do not easily lose their heads.

*　　　*　　　*

Pierre: Well, well, well, well! Whew! I never heard anything quite so jumbled and untrue in my life. You first say city life is bad and then conclude that it is good; you envy the lot of the farmer and then deplore it; you say the village life is peaceful and then that it is only the city in miniature. I haven't the slightest notion of what you really believe, and I doubt whether you have.

The Author: There you go again! What you lack more than anything else is refinement. You have never learned that all truths are comparative except fundamental truths, and no one knows what the fundamental truths are. You think a subject of this sort can be treated as though it were either all black or all white. Your criticism is about as helpful as a punch in the jaw.

Pierre: Maybe so, maybe so! Well, anyway my life as compared with yours is much more simple. You appear to have a lot to think about. As for me—give me a tranquil life. Let me be ignorant of comparative truth, and let me be unrefined.

*　　　*　　　*

During our day in camp we had frequently discussed the further course of our journey. There was still more of the Sandwich Range to the west—the sharp summit of Tripyramid which pokes a knife-edge of granite in the sky, and the rounded dome of Sandwich Mountain, gentle and graceful, though recently shorn quite bare by the lumber merchant. But northward rose the Presidential Range, monarchs of the White Mountains, and crowned by the rugged peak of Mt. Washington, where we hoped soon to be. I knew the Sandwich Range from previous journeys, and also the Presidential; but between lay a country strange to both of us, plotted on the map, but to us quite unreported. We examined the contours, measured the distances, traced the trails, and wondered what adventure might be in store for us in such plain country. More than the map could specify, for adventure lies as much inside the head as outside it.

When we awoke on Thursday morning a mountain fog was trailing through the trees, hiding all the shaggy head of Passaconaway above us, enveloping the trees in sombre mystery, tinging life with poetical softness. It was a fitting day for exploration.

We did not get under way promptly, as railroad trains pull out on time regardless of the conductor's disposition. On the contrary, until we had actually left camp under full marching-equipment, we were not certain of starting at all. A day in camp had tempered our ambition; and besides, the weather was constantly in doubt. During breakfast the fog had lifted, but it did not dissolve; long fingers were lapping towards the summit of Whiteface from the bowl, and the sky was heavy with dark clouds. We put off the lugubrious business of packing; we sat in the doorway of the camp and discussed the weather indolently. For in rainy weather it is well to have a roof over one's head, and the roofs in the woods between Passaconaway and the Presidential Range were probably few and at least uncertain. Our campmates lingered about the fire, politely urging us to wait another day. But at ten o'clock we packed our duffles; a half-hour later we started up the trail towards the tip of Passaconaway.

Carrying packs, as this book has already affirmed, is no business for gentlemen. All such had best hire porters for these humiliating pursuits and free the back as completely as the mind. Rousseau passes for a philosopher of nature, in the classroom if not in the open. Give ear to his precious philosophy: "Walking animates and enlivens my spirits; I can hardly think when in a state of inactivity; my body must be exercised to make my judgment active . . . I dispose of all nature as I please; my heart, wandering from object to object, approximates and unites with those that please it, is surrounded by charming images, and becomes intoxicated with delicious sensations." And of the other penmen who burst into raptures over the out-of-doors—Sterne, Hazlitt, Stevenson, Borrow—it is doubtful whether they essayed a mountain trail with a lurching, forty-pound handicap at their backs. Unlike Rousseau, as we went at this last five hundred feet of Passaconaway, we were not intoxicated with "delicious sensations." On the contrary, we were overwhelmed with shortness of breath and a heart palpitation which seemed as though it must be audible twenty rods away.

Passaconaway grows spruce woods to the very tip; views of the surrounding territory are to be had only from two open ledges on the west and on the east. In due time we had climbed to the eastern look-out, 4,116 feet above the sea. The view was as dark as the clouds. The peak of Chocorua had withdrawn from the gaze of human eyes whilst the weather gods held council there. In the midst of a dull landscape Chocorua Lake shone like a pot of molten silver. Bands of dim sunshine illumined the north slopes of Paugus and the fertile fields of Albany Intervale. But the summit of Passaconaway was cold and moist. We lingered there, free of our packs, smoking, and surveying the country to the north where our journey lay. We were in no mood for expedition, but it was the better part of wisdom to have daylight for walking; and at length, with noontide nearly on us, we took the trail marked "Albany Intervale."

And it was no holiday promenade, this Albany trail down the northern side of Passaconaway. In four days in the mountains we had ventured far, but we had not yet descended on the shoot of a landslide, down a broad path of rock polished smooth by streams of water. Such was the way to Albany Intervale. One might as well let one's pack slide down at the end of a rope, from parapet to parapet, and follow unencumbered. But we had no rope and no imagination either; so we dug our hobnails into every crevice, clung to the tiny spruces and birches which grow in the fissures, and descended cautiously, resting our nerves meanwhile by frequent pauses. In the haze to the north rose the Presidential peaks, mysterious mountains so far away. It was difficult to believe that we might cross all the intervening country on foot and still go that far before the holidays were over.

⁑   ⁑   ⁑

Pierre: Those are beautiful mountains 'way over there. It seems to me the basest sort of covetousness to want to climb them. Familiarity breeds contempt, old man. If we want to respect those mountains we ought to remain right where we are. It is sheer spiritual impudence to go another foot.

The Author: My friend, wherever human feet have trod we go unprotesting. *En avant!* May the devil take him who first cries, "Hold, enough!"

⁑   ⁑   ⁑

Half-way down the slide a tiny stream came from the woods to the west, crooning softly and trickling in shallow green pools where the ledges were flat like tables. We stopped to drink, to rest and to watch the clouds rise above the Presidentials on the northern sky-line. And lunch-time being close at hand we followed this same brook back into the woods to a broad basin, cool and shaded; and there, close by the water, we built a fire and cooked a meal. Then for the fourth or fifth time within two hours we sprawled on our backs, with the colour of the sky in our eyes, listening meanwhile to the running water. The afternoon was well along before we started down the slide again.

By two o'clock we had descended to the forest level where we pushed on swiftly through a thick growth of bushes. Once out of this tangle and on a lumber road we felt merry once more, and burst into a bastard sort of song, a pot-pourri of whistling and balladry which would have astonished alien ears. Once we came to a blueberry-patch where myriads of large, firm berries streaked the colour of the sky across the ground. It was late—absurdly late—but we could not resist them. We filled two empty cracker-tins with berries and for several mornings thereafter enjoyed the luxury of blueberries with hot oatmeal. Then on again, swiftly and boisterously, until at three o'clock we came out at Albany Intervale with less than half the day's scheduled journey behind.

III

HAVING been in the woods nearly five days, we felt the need of readjustment when we came to the sandy road. For although this end of Swift River Intervale is no metropolis, supports no store, no houses except Swift River Inn and its cottages, the manners of the woods are clearly not the manners of summer resorts. The trail to Sawyer Pond, whither we were bound, left the road a mile to the east; thus we should be in the woods again very quickly. But since our store of provisions had begun to dwindle more rapidly than we had anticipated, we hoped to make our enforced invasion of civilization profitable by replenishing our supply of bacon, rice and sugar. There were women on the veranda of Swift River Inn. And as we approached them what self-confidence we had been sedulously cultivating trickled mockingly away. What sort of preparation for the impeccable society of females are five days in the woods?

* * *

The Author: Don't you suppose we can get on without provisions for a day or two longer?

Pierre: Buck up, old man! You don't know these women, do you? You're much too self-conscious. We look rough, but we can be exceedingly refined in our address. Use the future conditional; that's the most refined in our language. Don't say, "Can we buy some provisions?" or "May we?" but "Would it be possible to buy provisions here?"

* * *

And lo! it was so. We removed our hats with a refined, modest flourish and fell at once into the future conditional. No sooner had we asked for provisions than the hostess of the Inn supplied them, while the summer guests (like recluses, eager to hear about the world) plied us with questions about our trip and our plans. One tested the weight of a pack but could not lift it from the ground. We were not distressed by her failure. It is said that the masculine sex is conceited. To which we reply, "And why not?"

Sawyer Pond lies five miles in the woods north of Swift River Intervale by a U.S. Forest Service trail which ascends a small ridge between Green's Cliff and Birch Hill, and then drops to the pond (1,790 feet) just behind Mt. Tremont and Owl Cliff. We forded Swift River and began a tedious and mo-

notonous walk, resting frequently to ease our shoulders and speculate on the distance. It was a steady, grinding progress, unrewarded by views or striking beauty. Once we passed two porcupines: they tumbled out of the way indifferently. At a small tributary to Rob Brook we saw a deer leap into the woods; tracks in the mud showed that she had been drinking at the brook before we came into sight. We reached a soggy shore of Sawyer Pond at 6:45. The sky was overcast; dusk was already tempering the day.

Sawyer Pond is the usual New Hampshire mountain lake, a few acres in area, boggy and marshy, and thick all around with a tangle of tough alders. We were not only weary and sullen, but anxious to find a camping-site without delay and to settle for the night. Half-way across the pond, on the opposite shore, was what appeared to be a high knoll. We started hurriedly around the southern shore, ready to walk to the knoll if no other spot seemed favourable. What evil spirits haunt the shores of mountain ponds? Why do they vex the shores with bogs and thickets? *Ah! Coquin de sort!* For a half-hour we struggled along the shore in bushes above our waists, sloshing through the marshes, stumbling over concealed sticks and at last cursing until the echoes rang. Then, pushing out to the pond, we found we were scarcely more than half-way to our knoll, while night was coming fast.

* * *

The Author: Damn these bushes! Let's sit down and smoke.

Pierre: The best suggestion yet. What I want to know is who proposed that we come here? Who ever heard of this blasted pond anyway?

The Author: "By the pricking of my thumbs
  Something wicked this way comes."

Pierre: "Double, double, toil and trouble,
  Fire burn and cauldron bubble."

The Author: By Juno, Euthydemus, nothing is accomplished by by this sort of going.

Pierre: It seems so to me, O Socrates! We aren't making any progress this way. By Jupiter, Socrates, let us take off our boots and stockings and wade along the edge of the shore.

* * *

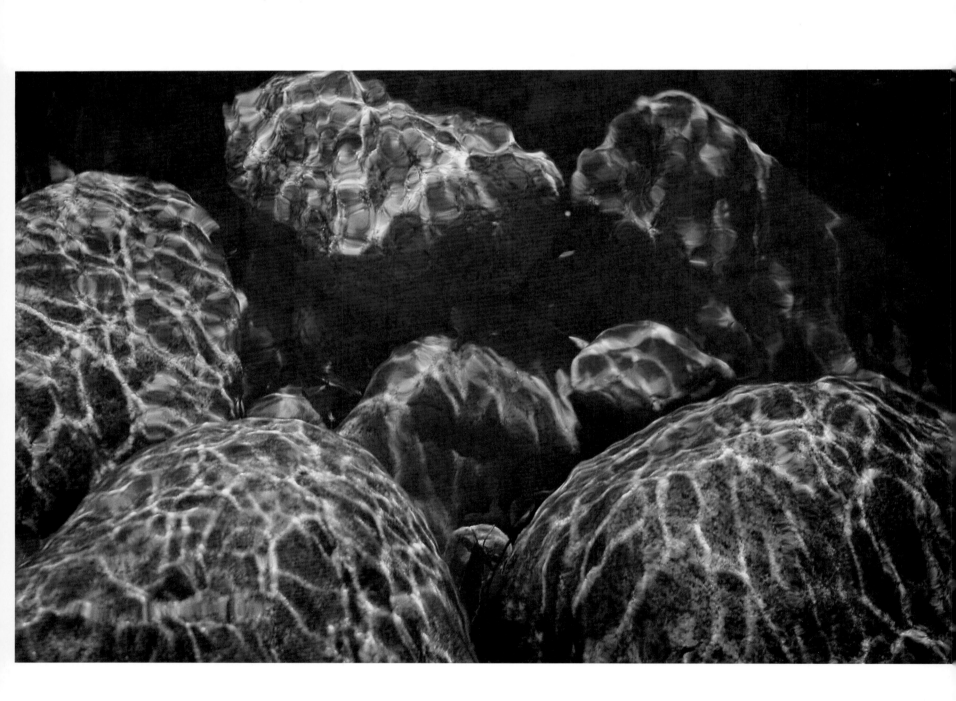

An admirable proposal! We pulled off our boots, tied them together, thrust the stockings inside, and began to wade close to the shore, feeling the icy cold of water near the inlets, and elsewhere the warmth of water which had rested all day in the sunlight. So we progressed nearly two rods until the bottom of the pond fell away into melancholy depths while the shore receded into a deep cove between us and the knoll for which we were leading. It was now my turn to make a suggestion. We had just passed three or four water-soaked logs on which were four loose boards, apparently in years past some fisherman's raft. I proposed that we ride on it majestically to yonder port. Upon testing its buoyancy, however, we found that while it would hold our packs, it sank when we crept aboard. *Semper pro impedimenta!* We decided to give our packs a voyage, and began to push the laden raft close by the shore. All went well until we reached deep water again.

*   *   *

The Author: By Jove, Euthydemus, nothing is accomplished by this sort of going.

Pierre: Great God of Russia! Let's take off all our clothes and push the damned raft straight across to the point.

*   *   *

And we did so. Removing all our adornments except the barest necessities—our glasses and pipes—we started swimming and smoking, pushing the raft steadily towards the knoll, the night meanwhile setting in black. It must have been eight o'clock when the raft gently bumped the rocks a hundred feet from the knoll on which we had pinned our faith. Mt. Tremont, rising steeply on the left, was faintly suggested against the sky. While Pierre steadied the raft I ferried our household goods through waist-high water to the shore, stepping cautiously over the rocky bottom to avoid dropping them in the water. After several trips our baggage was all ashore. Standing on a flat rock we rubbed dry and warm, well-pleased with our little adventure.

Why should we be in such a good humour? Why were we not as blasphemous as army officers? We were already tired after a long day's tramp over fairly commonplace country. We had been out of sorts when we found the shores of the pond so boggy and confused with rank bushes. We were hungry. The prospects of making camp and cooking supper in the darkness were by no means inviting. Moreover, the knoll to which we had come was almost as thick with bushes as the shores we had struggled to penetrate; its only advantage was the absence of bog. Surely no great cause for merriment! Yet the variety of our approach, together with the consciousness of having reached the end of our journey, put us in such high spirits that the drowsy pond awoke to the echoes of human laughter. In that dynamic mood we should have been discouraged by nothing.

At the top of the knoll was a sandy spot, about ten feet square, where we might be free of bushes. We carried the packs up the hill-side through evergreen bushes that scraped our bare legs, and while Pierre built a fire of dry roots which burned fiercely as soon as the match was applied, I stumbled down the bushy hill in the darkness to fill our kettles with water. From the shore of the pond the red glow of the fire on Pierre and a lone spruce behind him was a most cheerful sight. After supper we tried the echoes toward Mt. Tremont. The voices of the mountains flung back our shouts like solemn giants, speaking in quick succession and concluding in a faint, whispering monotone. Black as the night was, and starless, we could still see the dim flash of the pond, the outline of Green's Cliff beyond, and the ridges of Mt. Tremont rising ominously behind. Thunder began to roll to the north. The knoll was so homelike that we had nearly forgotten that we had no roof over our heads. We put several sticks on the fire and decided to get what sleep we could at once and then get up again to protect our packs with ponchos when the rain came. A barrel owl, or perhaps a great-horned owl, hooted twice mysteriously from the far shore. Meanwhile came a tremulous call, like a siren, rising quickly up the scale. We heard it several times but did not know what it could be. At 3:30 the next morning rain spattering in our faces woke us and we got up according to the plans, but fifteen minutes later it stopped. Returning to our blankets we slept soundly until 6:30.

You commonly make your camp just at sundown, and are collecting wood, getting your supper, or pitching your tent while the shades of night are gathering around and adding to the already dense gloom of the forest. You have no time to explore or look around you before it is dark. You may penetrate half a dozen rods farther into that twilight wilderness, after some dry bark to kindle your fire with, and wonder what mysteries lie hidden still deeper in it, say at the end of a long day's walk; or you may run down to the shore for a dipper of water, and get a clearer view for a short distance up or down the stream, and while you stand there, see a fish leap, or duck alight in the river, or hear a woodthrush or robin sing in the woods. That is as if you had been to town or civilized parts. But there is no sauntering off to see the country, and ten or fifteen rods seems a great way from your companions, and you come back with the air of a much travelled man, as from a long journey, with adventures to relate, though you may have heard the crackling of the fire all the while,—and at a hundred rods you might be lost past recovery, and have to camp out. It is all mossy and *moosey*. In some of those dense fir and spruce woods there is hardly room for the smoke to go up. The trees are a *standing* night, and every fir and spruce which you fell is a plume plucked from night's raven wing. Then at night the general stillness is more impressive than any sound, but occasionally you hear the note of an owl farther or nearer in the woods, and if near a lake, the semi-human cry of the loons at their unearthly revels.

—Henry David Thoreau

BY DAYLIGHT Sawyer Pond was more beautiful—although, like all small mountain ponds, a little lonely, pitiful and *triste*. Everywhere the woods marched down to the shores in mass formation, defiantly, as though they might choke the pond out of existence. The surface was nevertheless placid. But we abandoned our project for pushing north to Nancy Pond. (*Pierre:* To hell with ponds! Let's strike for the mountains.) By a journey of eleven miles, two of them along the state road, we might reach Camp Resolution, high on the Montalban Ridge, before night. But there were difficulties as yet unknown and unconsidered. After breakfast we explored the knoll we had reached in the darkness. Looking towards Mt. Tremont, Pierre suddenly let out a savage howl: "Good God! we're on an island." And so we were! What had seemed to be a cove in the gloom of the previous evening was in truth the shore of the pond, and we were now separated from the mainland by two or three hundred feet. So in human life impatient people fancy they have found a short cut to happiness when they are really poking into a *cul de sac*. Like the Cheeryble Brothers, who were always laughing pleasantly together (and sometimes seemed rather asinine), we set up a shout at this new turn of fortune. The raft was still where we had left it, but the stretch of water between the shore and the island looked shallow enough to be forded. We carried our baggage to a point nearest the mainland and took off our clothes again. The bottom of the pond was muddy, sending up dark whirls of muck wherever we stepped. And although the water was deeper than we had anticipated we found one route where it was never above our shoulders. First we carried our clothes across experimentally. After all they were the least valuable part of the cargo. Returning to the island we swung our packs lengthwise against the backs of our necks and carried them cautiously to shore. Then taking advantage of the situation we went back into the water for a bit of a swim. The first white-throated sparrow we had heard was singing on the island, but clearly the flush of

spring had gone by, for according to his midsummer manner he flatted the last few notes of his song and lost its distinguishing freshness. Again we were on our way, climbed the steep edge of Mt. Tremont through the woods and found an abandoned lumber road which we followed two miles through wet and rugged woods to the Carrigain-Livermore logging railroad. Once when we sat down to repair a pair of broken spectacles a magnolia warbler flew into a near-by tree. Most beautiful of the warblers, a gay fellow of black, yellow and white, he was as pleasing as the crossbills on Passaconaway.

By eleven o'clock we were fairly out of the woods in Livermore, a lumber village supporting a railroad, a steam sawmill and a hundred men who live with their families in frame houses with sharp-peaked roofs—all as plain and as similar as the people who live inside them. Sheltered by rugged hills, sung to by a broad mountain torrent, the people of Livermore might live in a spot of rare beauty. But as mechanically as they saw trees and load the boards on railroad cars, they have built their unlovely houses in plain rows, after the fashion of city tenement districts; and they have cut down all the trees which might shelter them from the baking sun of August. The dreariness and wretchedness of their village are undisguised. With the sawmill screaming for more logs, the people have no time for beauty or living. And how can children learn to distinguish beauty from ugliness in such surroundings? As if to prove the point of our reflections, the lad of thirteen or fourteen years who tended the camp-store spoke as foully as the grown men outside. We made our purchases of bacon, beans, crackers and matches and set out down the road for Sawyer's River, glad to shake Livermore dust from our boots. We rode the two miles to Bemis in an automobile as guests of a generous-minded woman driver who happened to pass our way. Then after crossing the Saco River we plunged into the woods again and climbed to the Montalban Ridge which runs fifteen sky-line miles to the summit of Mt. Washington. Once

more we were high in the mountains; they tumbled precipitously into Crawford Notch, losing their outlines in the blue haze which marked the winding course of that deep pass.

*   *   *

Pierre: Well, I feel safe again. I was almost afraid of being seduced during those two miles of highway.

The Author: Seduced?

Pierre: Yes, seduced. After five or six days in the woods I was afraid I might be debauched by an automobile or the smell of a steak cooking in some kitchen or the sight of a feather-bed. But I was not even tempted. My virtue is assured. In fact, I was offended by the sight of roads and houses and disgusted by the automobiles and their smug passengers. They were chugging along as though they were enjoying the mountains.

The Author: As far as that goes, we think we are enjoying the mountains. What's the difference?

Pierre: The difference, my dear fellow, is that we *know* we are enjoying them. And if that does not please your sense of impartiality, let me point out gently that we have been in the mountains and know what they are; whereas all those blackguards know about the mountains is that they have to shift gears on the steepest hills. If we are not more holy than they, then I'm a Piccadilly dandy and you're the Crown Prince of Monaco.

*   *   *

The day was intolerably humid, of a piece with all the weather since our journey began. And thunder which had grumbled across Sawyer Pond the evening before had continued all night and morning. As we set foot on the summit of Mt. Crawford, thunder rolled across the northern mountains in a long, reverberating discord. Such thunder as that one must take seriously. We rinsed our parched throats in the brackish water which lay in fissures of the rocky summit, rested discreetly, rejoiced again to be so far above the lowlands, and started towards Camp Resolution for shelter from the threatening storm.

For the first few miles the Montalban Ridge is partly bare and partly grown to spruces. We dipped through several dark hollows crowded with small trees and crossed open spaces where we might look off, regard the landmarks and gauge our progress. The gods once played at bowls here, with no lack of implements; huge boulders were sprinkled all over the crest where these superhuman players had left them. And when they were all in the frolic the game must have been as thunderous as the northern sky, which was growing constantly more threatening. We passed Crawford Dome without venturing to the summit and crossed to a shoulder of Mt. Resolution. And almost before we realized how far the path had led us we were at the turning which drops abruptly off the ridge to Camp Resolution. Thrice welcome, indeed, was the roof of that shelter, a hundred feet below.

We scrambled down breathlessly, tumbled the packs into camp and flung ourselves on the spruce bedding, exhausted. A half-hour must have passed while we lay there, our eyes closed and our minds full of dreamy content. "Hallo!" Pierre exclaimed, looking into a dark corner. Hallo, indeed! For there was a porcupine, squeezing himself behind a pile of fire-wood. Nine days in every ten, Camp Resolution is no doubt his; we were the real intruders, and not he. But by means of a stick we indicated that for the present at least Camp Resolution could

no longer provide him with shelter; and bristling all over and grunting a manner of bestial protest he climbed up the far wall to the roof. Here was an impasse indeed. We poked; he clung to the logs, hissing and affecting a vicious attitude. But at last by combining our strength we tore him loose, and he ran out the unguarded corner of the camp. It is curious how the superstition persists that porcupines can shoot their quills. Even in the arid wastes of the Arabian desert the Bedouins cling to that belief. In his masterpiece of travel books, "Arabia Deserta," C. M. Doughty makes note of that: "It is also the Arab's fable," he writes, "that the creature can shoot out his pricks against an enemy." Yet no wild beast is less offensive than these gauche animals, forever grunting and nosing about in quest of salt and grease. Their quilled backs protect them well—almost too well. For unless one attacks them viciously, porcupines never make haste to get away. They are not so obliging. But let no one suppose that these clumsy movements are all of which they are capable. No; they are merely lazy. Attack them to some purpose, with a savage yell or two, and they fly off almost as rapidly as rabbits.

While thunder still echoed to the north and began to roar also in the east, as though two storms were coming together, we cooked our supper, washed in the brook below the camp, in icy water which left us entirely refreshed, lighted our pipes, and as evening fell gradually, we stood on the ledge before camp, looking at the huge, towering cliffs of Giant Stairs behind us, or north-west over mountain ridges to Webster, miles of spruce forest lying between—a vast panorama, far too extensive, far too varied, far too rich to be tasted in what time we had to spare.

The two storms approached; they would meet, it seemed, over this ridge of mountains. Towards eight o'clock the thunder increased in volume, a succession of long reverberations which which shook the ground, while flashes of lightning lit up the woods and mountains like the brightest glare of noon-time. As the wind increased in fury, bending the tops of spruce-trees, whistling and whining through their branches, we made camp cosy for the night. By 8:30 the storm broke. Lightning snapped all around us. Thunder shook the camp and "ripped with rubato rage." The wind now blew furiously; rain swept viciously over the roof. Grateful for shelter and security, we crept into the sleeping-bags, watching the fire struggle with the rain. It was a glorious storm. But we fell asleep long before the skies had cleared.

Indeed, we slept eleven hours that night. When I awoke on Saturday morning the hands of the watch pointed to 8:15. And while I yawned and stretched, a junco flew into the camp, and an American crossbill flew into the fire-place in search of food. The red of his plumage was brilliant enough to kindle the fire, and would that he had done so! For if the whole truth must be set down in this volume, we made a sorry business of that morning and risked the whole promenade.

Some soporific old wind-bag has said: "Look after the morning until nine o'clock and the rest of the day will look after itself." One is reluctant to subscribe to such doctrines, perhaps only because so many others do. But despite all that the early hours are critical. Now, after a soaking rain-storm any fool knows that open fires cannot be kindled casually. I knew that,

on this Saturday morning in August, after eleven full hours of sleeping; but still I went about this business indifferently. A few sticks caught and held a flame, but the fire did not flourish, and the sleepy builder did nothing to stimulate it. Our dispositions rose and fell with the heat. After the oatmeal had cooked somewhat sluggishly the blaze shrank to a smoulder too weak for cooking griddles. I refused to believe it and poured batter into the pan; the cake stuck to the bottom, however, and crumpled when I tried to flip it over. Pierre delivered a long and perfidious malediction; and as for me, I was too ashamed to say a word. We ate the oatmeal phlegmatically, quite without relish, and conversation expired with the last gasp of flame. So breakfast lasted from nine to eleven.

"Come on," I said, "and get this fire burning before we murder each other."

Pierre indicated that he could not honestly forswear murder, even with the fire crackling merrily. It was, indeed, high time for action.

We climbed up above the camp clearing to some birch-trees where bark was hanging in long strips. Two armfuls of this would be sufficient for a Saturnalian feast. In the woods to the west I found a dead birch which I cut and split and a standing spruce which I prepared in the same fashion. Meanwhile Pierre had collected an abundance of kindling. We laid the sticks carefully, stacked the damp wood all around, and applied a match in several places. Lo! the fire was soon roaring—snapping and sizzling hot all the rest of the day.

*   *   *

Pierre: Thank God for our immortal souls.

The Author: Thank God for our stock of provisions.

Pierre: They don't count. I agree with the Russian intellectuals, that nothing matters but the immortal soul.

The Author: I notice that you make that profound observation while your stomach is full, the sun is pleasantly warm, and you are smoking your first pipe for the day.

Pierre: Pardon me for using an unfair argument, but O hell! The soul lives independent of the body. Starve the body or freeze it; but you do not harm the soul. You are a bourgeois. No good will come to the world from such as you. Your immortal soul is about as sweet and juicy as a sheet of wrapping-paper.

*   *   *

Amid the rumble of exhortation which is forever ringing in the ears of growing children it is at once noticeable and deplorable that so little heed is given to the rare art of failing successfully. Pure success draws all the claqueurs. Parents who have felt the pinch of life and seen in retrospect how narrowly they missed filling the secret chest with doubloons are eager that their children shall not leave the main highway at precisely the same point. Well-provided citizens of the town strut up and down the public-school platforms with a manner instinctively dignified, and dribble platitudes about success while the hands of the clock stand still. Business men of prominence and influence consent to write their formulas for success in the popular magazines. The life of Abraham Lincoln is searched for its secret and unrolled before the wondering eyes of schoolchildren with scant respect for its spiritual qualities. Benjamin Franklin's "Autobiography" is "put into" the schools for its good example: "Be-

cause it is sound advice, sir; no nonsense about it," as the school committee-men say with a twirl of their huge mustachios. Life is thus pictured a gruelling race up a steep hill; he who lingers by the wayside to tie his shoe, to sip at a gurgling brook, or to admire the graceful curve of distant hills and valleys—is lost!

Humbug! There have been and still are some who climb the hill not by the main highway but by dim, twisting paths which wander through the forest; not at a steady, muscle-wearying pace, but leisurely, or with intermittent bursts of speed which are rewarded by long rests beside the streams. Occasionally they are "the cool persons in the meadows by the wayside" whom Stevenson observed "lying with a handkerchief over their ears and a glass at their elbows." At times they poke out on the bare ridges, recline indolently (some say insolently) at full length and watch the perspiring stream on the main highway below and above them. For they are invariably passed. Only an occasional one finds the way to the top—and then absurdly late. They are not successes. Surely they are not failures. They are a blend of the two—successful failures.

It is recorded that when the rich and brilliant Alexander the Great, King of Greece, Persia, Egypt—nay, a god, duly enrolled among the sacred deities of all the cities of his great empire, asked Diogenes to name his greatest wish, the tub-dweller replied simply: "Do not stand between me and the sun." Ribaldry —sheer ribaldry from the lips of one whose possessions numbered only a cloak and a wallet, and a wooden bowl which he discarded as superfluous when he saw a boy drink from the hollow of his hands. "To want nothing is divine," said Socrates, the snub-nosed; "to want as little as possible is the nearest approach to the divine life." Emerson wrote of Thoreau: "He chose to be rich by making his wants few." Forsooth, an unostentatious sort of men who need not be reckoned as disputers of the spoils which are reported to lie in glittering abundance at the summit of the mountain.

One would expect such folk to be left undisturbed on their points of vantage in the same measure that they avoid disturbing the eager runners on the beaten road. For long periods they lie so motionless that they seem parts of the landscape and are mistaken for rocks or trees by the unsuspecting throng. They do not thrust themselves presumptuously upon the crowd; they do not bustle importantly into public meetings and argue from the floor; they do not seize every occasion to mount the soapbox, clear their throats and burst into a quivering torrent of rhetorical abuse. Lambs could be no less ferocious or prying. In truth, their most serious intrusions are a book or two which may be ignored by leaving them unopened on the bookstands. Yet it is noticeable that if one of the passionate runners on the highway stops to fling a chance jeer at the loafer on the nearest ridge (thereby clearing his mind), his fellows soon join in the baiting. They form an irate throng, shake their fists in anger, fume and bellow as though this silent figure had maliciously slandered them. Socrates, who walked the streets of Greece harmlessly, speaking only when spoken to, a modest man, painfully conscious of his own want of learning and his own limitations, yet drew the displeasure of so petty a politician as Meletus and was condemned by a cynical assembly to the cup of hemlock. Thus conscience does make cowards of us all!

FOR ONCE, THEN, SOMETHING

Others taunt me with having knelt at well-curbs
Always wrong to the light, so never seeing
Deeper down in the well than where the water
Gives me back in a shining surface picture
Me myself in the summer heaven godlike
Looking out of a wreath of fern and cloud puffs.
Once, when trying with chin against a well-curb,
I discerned, as I thought, beyond the picture,
Through the picture, a something white, uncertain,
Something more of the depths—and then I lost it.
Water came to rebuke the too clear water.
One drop fell from a fern, and lo, a ripple
Shook whatever it was lay there at bottom,
Blurred it, blotted it out. What was that whiteness?
Truth? A pebble of quartz? For once, then, something.

—ROBERT FROST

There is no startling originality in the thought that a man cannot be all things at once. Those who choose to idle away languorous hours in the cool shade, dreaming or playing the lute, cannot look forward to the rococo splendour of palaces on the summit. At best they can only suck up every drop of the present and argue that the castles do not exist. Neither can the runners on the main highway "loaf and invite their souls." Devoting all their energy and all their time to the race, for it is a close one, they must expect to become a trifle dull—be, like the Monk's horse, "gode . . . but nat gay."

The runners on the highway stick close together, not only in their contempt for loiterers, but also in their admiration of themselves. Insidious suggestions that the common reports (on which the race has been founded) grossly exaggerate the amount of treasure on the summit, or that the palaces after all may be nothing but tawdry pieces of architecture, give them a moment's sceptical uneasiness, but nothing more. They push on relentlessly, their faces set grim. In good time their hearts drop into their stomachs, as did Adrian Harley's, "where it was much lighter, nay, an inspiring weight, and encouraged him merrily on." Where the grade climbs steepest they whip their protesting flesh with glaring sign-boards: "Damn your excuses! We want results." "In God we trust; all others cash." "To be good is well, to do good is better; to 'make good' is best." Refreshment booths along the way sell not sparkling wines or delicately tinted liqueurs but lithographed pamphlets whose covers scream,

"You can!" Demagogues of the racing tribe who are said to have reached the top and to have strolled back altruistically to assist those still on the way lay bare in such writings the secrets of personality, memory and persistence which are said to win the race. What though a pallor renders their cheeks lifeless, though their eyes glare like those of caged lions, though they jump nervously at every noise? A time will come, they tell themselves, when they can seek their affluent ease in garrulous coffeehouses where gossip and politics pass the time pleasantly away.

Meanwhile, sheltered from the glare of the baking sun and sung to by silvery mountain streams, the loafers go on musing and dreaming. Their clothes are not dusty with the grime of the highway but fragrant with the odours of wild flowers which blossom on woodsy banks. While the contestants in the race are eternally buoying up their spirits with thoughts of the golden-paved summits, the idlers are whistling lazy tunes, their hands clasped behind their backs, and attending to the business of humanity. They are "such honest, civil, quiet men!" They wonder whether the "You can!" books, whose gaudy lithographing they can read at long range and which teach the art of "selling oneself," do not smell somewhat of the oldest profession in the world. Efficiency they do not comprehend. Fear they know not—nor jealousy nor hysteria. Their conscience pricks them only when they lose themselves. A serious assertion such as Dudley Warner's that snow-storms "take away the sin of idleness by making it a necessity" is to them the barest buncombe.

. . . A being rushes past us, heated, breathless, blind of Nature's beauty. He looks straight before him, watch in hand. "Two hours, fourteen minutes, forty seconds," he cries in triumph as he hastens by. An anxious moment for us, who took four hours! Is this a herald of disaster in the valley? By no means; it is the speed-merchant, the record-breaker. Brevity is the soul of his pleasure and success. This fleeting man is the representative of a whole class. He disappears for a moment into the hotel, presumably to publish his feat, then dashes off for the summit in search of further records. Perhaps he brings off his coup, and catches the first train home; ours is the last train, so we shall have no chance of lamenting to him that he has seen so much less than we have, and sped by so much beauty unnoticed. But perhaps he would have regarded us with an uncomprehending disdain. These man are the proudest and most exclusive of climbers. The slow mover, it is true, has reason for modesty, but he may well be the happier. The record-breaker can never find a true, calm happiness, for almost always there comes one bolder, cleverer, quicker, to outbid him. Hence arises the vile, competitive spirit of the market-place. But no man can outbid you or rob you of that love of nature and its mountains, which burns silent within your heart. Hold fast to that which is good.

—Julius Kugy

The idlers on the ridges whisper that some who have raced to the summit found the luxury suffocating and so at length drifted below the tree-line where vegetation flourishes. Others report that the talk there runs free only a few months before it begins to repeat, that those who have moved into the richest houses go blind from the glitter of the gold and jewels, that the very paths for casual strolling are laid in circles and the boldest promenades thus return in good time to their starting-points. The coffee-houses are described as stiff places of cold formality. They say that the muscles which grow hard during the race are soon flabby from want of exercise. Even the bright hopes which during the race fill the minds of the contestants with kaleidoscopic pictures soon die and leave them wizened blanks.

Such news is drowned by the noise of the race. A censorship has been established to keep the bearers of ill tidings from the refreshment booths where the "how to" booklets are sold. For a man cannot run well unless his heart is in the race. Perhaps that is why the contestants brand dissenters as snobs, prigs, knaves, blackguards and braggadocios, to strengthen their own morale. After all, who knows but that they are right? Who knows but the news from the summit is hopelessly prevaricated, that the idlers are foxes after grapes, that activity is really its own reward, that "energistic teleology," as the pundits say, is more worthy than hedonism? "In the jumble of existence there must be many a shock and many a grief," writes George Santayana; "people living at cross-purposes cannot be free from malice, and they must needs be foiled by their pretentious passions. But there is no need of taking those evils tragically." Observers and contestants in the human race are prone to take such differences as tragedies. But when the heat radiates from the baking highway and bodies are weary from the race, the temper of the runners jumps on slight provocation. Meanwhile, it is cool and sweet in the woods.

*   *   *

Pierre: By Jupiter, literature is strange business!

The Author: Well, what now?

Pierre: As a general thing words are used for the exchange of ideas, and as far as possible every one tries to speak the same language. But in literature words are used merely so the author can pirouette a little to please his own vanity. You talk of "successful failures." Well, what the hell do you mean? I know what success is, and I know what failure is; and you can't persuade me that the two mean the same or that one meaning is interchangeable with the other. Come, let us have a little sense or let us have some blank pages where we can write down a word or two of some consequence.

The Author: Look here, my friend, I'm sure you don't require everything to be useful.

Pierre: You bet I do; and why not?

The Author: Well, haven't you a little room in this gigantic, teeming, bubbling bean of yours for a little nonsense now and then?

Pierre: Sure! If it's nonsense it's useful. Well?

The Author: Very well. Here's a little nonsense. What are you so excited about?

Pierre: A little nonsense? No, my boy, no. This is not nonsense. This is what the Sunday book reviewers call "mellow" literature. This is supposed to go with mulled ale, warden pipes, beer-stained benches and immodest wenches. Now, I can get on well enough with that sort of society, but when it gets mixed up with the aesthetic, I—

The Author: The nuances of art, the fragile, tenuous shades of—

Pierre: Blah, blah!

*   *   *

We put a kettle of prunes to stew over the fire and turned again to the volume of Socrates. Having read at Passaconaway Plato's account of Socrates' defence when he was on trial for not believing in the gods whom the city held sacred, but for designing to introduce other and new deities; and likewise for his having corrupted the youth, we now turned to Xenophon's defence of Socrates—less sublime in its translated style than Plato, but equally reverential. And if to the practical ears of moderns Socrates' apology before the court of five hundred and one seemed needlessly indiscreet, antagonizing and foolhardy, quite defeating the apparent purpose for which he made it, Xenophon convinced us of its true nobility—its courage, faith, its honourable consistency with the whole life of the speaker. The philosophers have several quarrels with the wisdom of Socrates; for, in truth, he was a pioneer; and like pioneers he did not achieve perfection. But the most cynical do not find in his life or teachings, as they have come down to us, the least sign of unworthy motives. He made many enemies among the politicians and sophists—Critias, Charicles, Hippias and Protagoras. But what seeker after truth does not? The progress of human civilization rests upon more sweaty speed than by their nature the teachings of Socrates provoke. What human civilizations achieve, however, does not reflect discredit upon the relative immobility of Socrates' thought. On the contrary, his insistence upon soundness of doctrine and knowledge among the law-makers and clearness of thought among the teachers shows the penalties we pay year by year for skimming over those virtues.

In reading this panegyric of Socrates and that most human and enlivening account of "The Banquet," we were pleasantly interrupted several times: a winter wren sang fairy music; a pine grosbeak perched in the sunshine in a tree above the camp and glowed with brilliant colour. Towards the end of the afternoon a brisk wind came up from the north-west, driving away the haze which had hung around the mountains for a week. Webster being the only distant mountain in view, it served as a measure of visibility. By five o'clock Webster was clear, dark blue. The wind was high and the temperature falling. Far into the evening we enjoyed a brisk camp-fire of split birch sticks and watched the stars flickering as they do on cold, clear evenings. By candlelight we finished reading "The Banquet" and went to bed.

More than a night went by before morning; a season passed as well. For a week summer had been making rather too much of her prerogatives, but during the night autumn burst across the mountains buoyantly and freshly. What a new world it was on Sunday morning! A vigorous wind came spanking out of the north-west, clearing the atmosphere to crystalline purity, and driving huge banks of cloud gaily along; they seemed to be just over our heads. The wind was cold against our faces as we got out of the protection of the cabin; we pulled on our sweaters and lighted the fire as quickly as possible. Indeed, a glorious morning, a spur to physical activity. For a half-hour before sunlight crept into the deep ravine where Camp Resolution is hidden, Giant Stairs loomed roseate above us. We tried the echoes in that direction. After each lusty shout they answered for six seconds, running down the valley to a whisper from the last ridge towards Crawford Notch. So we need not merely sublimate ourselves into Nature, but we could talk to her as well. She was as polyphonic on this bright morning as an orchestra.

We did not linger over our meal longer than was necessary, for there were views to be seen on a day like this from the many openings on the Montalban Ridge, always higher, always nearer Mt. Washington. We burst up the trail with alacrity, stopping once to pull off our sweaters but not again until we had "slabbed" up the sheer slope of Giant Stairs almost to the summit. It was too windy for most of the birds; they are silent in blustering weather. But the chickadee, as Emerson knew full well, is not less cheery because the skies do not smile with warmth; and at the side path to the head of Giant Stairs we heard one in the spruce-trees. Not the familiar chickadee of southern New England, however, whom Emerson celebrated in song; his note was less vibrant and his markings less bold. He was the Hudsonian titmouse, a northern brother, who lives in spruce forests in the mountains.

From the head of Giant Stairs the view was glorious, a cyclorama indeed with the clouds whipping on and foaming from the tips of the Franconia Mountains and from Carrigain; and almost a kaleidoscope with the variety of colours in the sky down towards the far horizon. Below us were the woods where we had spent a day in camp; Mt. Resolution rolled up and beyond. In the south the Sandwich Range, bulwark of the White Mountains, swung cleanly into the sky. Kancamagus, Osceola, Sandwich Dome, Tripyramid and Passaconaway were all clear of cloud, and the tip of Chocorua poked above Resolution. We sat down to survey the landscape through the glasses, picking out familiar details of house and road in Jackson, and following roughly our course from the Sandwich Range north by Sawyer Pond, which was hidden by intervening summits. Deer tracks, apparently two days old, recorded the visit of another climber who had ostensibly looked at this view also from the same position. We hoped that he made as much of it as we did.

TWO LOOK AT TWO

Love and forgetting might have carried them
A little further up the mountain side
With night so near, but not much further up.
They must have halted soon in any case
With thoughts of the path back, how rough it was
With rock and washout, and unsafe in darkness;
When they were halted by a tumbled wall
With barbed-wire binding. They stood facing this,
Spending what onward impulse they still had
In one last look the way they must not go,
On up the failing path, where, if a stone
Or earthslide moved at night, it moved itself;
No footstep moved it. 'This is all,' they sighed,
'Good-night to woods.' But not so; there was more.
A doe from round a spruce stood looking at them
Across the wall, as near the wall as they.
She saw them in their field, they her in hers.
The difficulty of seeing what stood still,
Like some up-ended boulder split in two,
Was in her clouded eyes: they saw no fear there.
She seemed to think that two thus they were safe.
Then, as if they were something that, though strange,
She could not trouble her mind with too long,
She sighed and passed unscared along the wall.
'This, then, is all. What more is there to ask?'
But no, not yet. A snort to bid them wait.
A buck from round the spruce stood looking at them
Across the wall as near the wall as they.
This was an antlered buck of lusty nostril,
Not the same doe come back into her place.
He viewed them quizzically with jerks of head,
As if to ask, 'Why don't you make some motion?
Or give some sign of life? Because you can't.
I doubt if you're as living as you look.'
Thus till he had them almost feeling dared
To stretch a proffering hand—and a spell-breaking.
Then he too passed unscared along the wall.
Two had seen two, whichever side you spoke from.
'This *must* be all.' It was all. Still they stood,
A great wave from it going over them,
As if the earth in one unlooked-for favor
Had made them certain earth returned their love.

—ROBERT FROST

IV

THIS was no longer the promenade begun gaspingly at Chocorua a week before. These were no longer the struggling, puffing humans who on that Sunday groaned under their packs. The change in the weather had enlivened our spirits; and the week of climbing in the mountains had toughened our shoulders and legs, and we followed the trail along the crest of the Montalban Ridge, facing the wind, in a jubilant mood. Over the crest of Giant Stairs we went, through a hollow watered by a spring and flourishing with rank weeds, through a burned area to the first of the several peaks of Mt. Davis.

A twist in the trail suddenly brought into view the southern peaks of the Mt. Washington Range. It was startling to come on them so sharply. We were not quite conscious for the first time that these were the mountains towards which we had been travelling; they are always the goal of White Mountain promenades. One may snivel if one chooses at the dominance of the highest mountain in a range, or the largest city in a country, or the tallest mechanical structure in the world. "No other monument since the cathedrals—perhaps since the pyramids—has so stirred human sensibility as the Eiffel Tower," wrote Remy de Gourmont scornfully. "Confronted with all that junk reared on high, stupidity itself became lyric, fools meditated, wild asses dreamed." But to defy the superlative is to defy a social instinct, and to accomplish that liberation is to reach the apotheosis of cerebralism. Not that the Presidential Range is more beautiful than the Sandwich Range, or more attractive. Those southern mountains are less celebrated and are less trammelled by the mob; the camper's life there is more secluded. Nevertheless, it is toward Mt. Washington that the tourist turns obediently, the cynosure of all eyes. How many a little hill in New Hampshire and Vermont basks in the reflected glory of being a "Mt. Washington look-out"! We were now in the neighbourhood of giants.

And they were struggling with other giants, with clouds which boiled over the summits and whipped across the intervening ravine on the wings of the wind. The scene was one of such physical activity, in majestic proportions, on such a mammoth scale that one could not be indifferent to it. As we followed the trail just under the summit-line of Mt. Davis, and always closer to the Presidentials, it was not long before we felt occasional sprays of cold mist on our faces. Here, indeed, was the warground of the gods whither it seemed foolhardy for mere humans to wander.

We climbed to the wind-swept dome of Mt. Davis for a broad view, one of the best in all the White Mountains. Now we could see all that was visible from Giant Stairs, and more as well—Baldface and Sable near Chatham; and far in the south beyond the Sandwich Range were several small mountains, perhaps Monadnock, Crotchet and their neighbours, invisible save on the most brilliant days. Chilled by the wind, which ran through the tiny spruces like fire in a grassy field, we soon turned back for shelter. But before we dropped down into the woods, Pierre cut one of these ankle-high trees which cover the tops of such exposed summits. A few rods from the top, in the midst of protecting woods, was an overturned spruce on which we could count the rings of yearly growth. The stump measured six inches across; the tree was fifty-nine years old. Through the microscope Pierre examined the specimen cut on the peak. It was five-eighths of an inch thick and twenty years old. There were doubtless others on top no larger but twice as old. And the miracle is not that they grow no larger, but that they grow at all. Somewhat numb from exposure to the wind, we built a large fire beside a spring to cook luncheon and to warm ourselves. It was a jolly sight to see the pan of beans bubbling and the coffee steaming. After eating we lingered gratefully about the flames, warming our stiff fingers—at noon-time in midsummer. The date was August; the weather, however, was November.

There were three or four miles yet through wild country to Camp Isolation, where we planned to spend the night. And the afternoon was bleak and greyish, swept with gusts of rain; tatters of cloud dashed across the peaks and swirled through the trees—an afternoon of furies. Before leaving the fire we pulled on our sweaters again and put the oilskins within easy reach. Our boots sank to the tops in marshy spots along the trail, but they kept dry inside; and we held our own against the elements. Beyond the last summit of Davis the trail bent to the left just under the top of Mt. Isolation and finally led us into a patch of burned forest.

Here was another "unfinished part of the world," or a part once finished, perhaps, but since violated, and now a natural monstrosity. It was piled with dead, twisted trees that fretted the dark sky with bleached fingers—a dismal confusion, the wilderness made wilder, the charm rubbed off, the hideous, the horrific laid on thick, an angry and truculent ruin, impossible to penetrate without trail or ax. Once upon a time man regarded all wild nature as a thing malevolent in this fashion; even now the emotion persists in such places of violence, and civilized man does not approach them with the same tranquility with which he walks through natural forest. Between blustering weather and burned forest the Montalban Ridge had a troubled and disturbing air. Yet to the south-east, twenty miles from the high mountains, the sky was deep blue and Mt. Pequaket was bright with sunshine. As we recovered our composure somewhat by looking in that direction, as though at a Promised Land, we saw the roof of Camp Isolation glistening with moisture in the midst of a dreary tangle. We found the path to it, almost too slight a line to follow. One muddy place in it bore the footprint of a bear; it was too much in harmony with the environment to thrill us or to seem as unusual as bear-prints are in the White

Mountains. As we scraped a way into camp through the last dead thicket a cold rain began pattering on the roof. The wind whipped down the ridge, burst round a ledge at the camp doorway, and kept the fire dancing and roaring, snapping with sparks and hissing with rain. Before supper was cooked our stack of wood was exhausted; in the gathering dusk we went in search of more fuel that was not too dead and hard for burning. After supper we both put on extra woollen shirts and also the sweaters and pulled the fire up close to camp, where its warmth was not carried off by the wind.

The talk that evening was serious and pretentious, too studied to be entirely honest.

*   *   *

Pierre: Sir, what good have you done to-day?

The Author: Speaking quite seriously, I can think of none. I have absorbed good every moment, but I can think of none given out. It seems presumptuous to say it, but if we do any good on such a trip as this, it is indirectly, developing ourselves in the woods to be better citizens at home. That is the best answer I can make.

Pierre: Your simplicity amuses me. Now if we accept Socrates' paradox that the highest knowledge is the knowledge of universal ignorance, is it not true that we have approached knowledge on this journey?

The Author: It seems so to me.

Pierre: By living in the woods, have we not learned to distinguish the transitory from the permanent, the ephemeral from the solid, better than we could before?

The Author: With that also I agree.

Pierre: Well, then, are we not at least potentially better citizens, capable of more good, than we were before?

The Author: How can it be otherwise?

*In the Great Gulf, 1924,
Pierre, left; Brooks, right
(photo taken by a string attached
to the camera).*

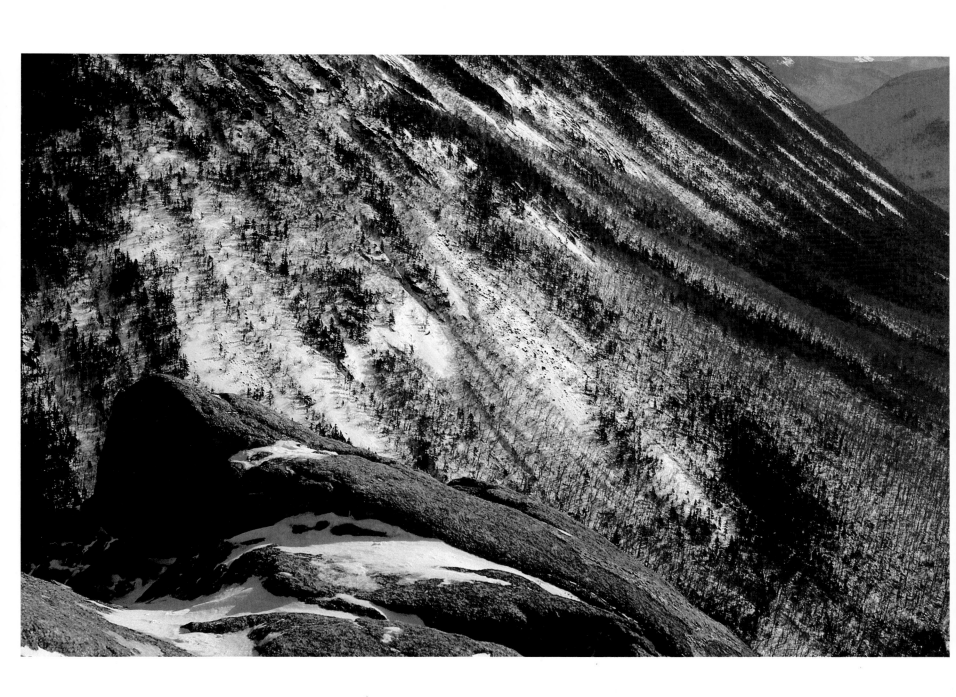

At length I entered within the skirts of the cloud which seemed forever drifting over the summit, and yet would never be gone, but was generated out of that pure air as fast as it flowed away: and when, a quarter of a mile farther, I reached the summit of the ridge, which those who have seen in clearer weather say is about five miles long, and contains a thousand acres of table-land, I was deep within the hostile ranks of clouds, and all objects were obscured by them. Now the wind would blow me out a yard of clear sunlight, wherein I stood; then a gray, dawning light was all it could accomplish, the cloud-line ever rising and falling with the wind's intensity. Sometimes it seemed as if the summit would be cleared in a few moments, and smile in sunshine: but what was gained on one side was lost on another. It was like sitting in a chimney and waiting for the smoke to blow away. It was, in fact, a cloud-factory,—these were the cloud-works, and the wind turned them off done from the cool, bare rocks.

—HENRY DAVID THOREAU

While the wind howled and dashes of rain swept across the roof we talked with amazing profundity of the nature of good. We talked, also, of happiness—a more popular topic; and of its unfortunate alliance with the good. After so much intellectual warmth it was astonishing to find how coldly we slept that night, although we were dressed in all the clothes we had and were buttoned tightly into blankets and ponchos. At the Summit House on Mt. Washington the temperature dropped to 31° and frosts whitened the lowlands as far south as Massachusetts, as we learned a few days later. We should have been glad of a few more civilized luxuries and superfluities that bleak night in Camp Isolation. "The philosopher is in advance of his age even in the outward form of his life," Thoreau wrote in "Walden." "He is not fed, sheltered, clothed, warmed like his contemporaries. How can a man be a philosopher and not maintain his vital heat by better methods than other men?" Clearly we were not philosophers, as we had chosen to dub ourselves. Our tepid vital heat betrayed our mongrel breed.

DURING the night the clouds lifted above Isolation and the Montalban Ridge, but did not disappear. On Monday morning they were still billowing majestically from the unseen summit of Mt. Washington. At five o'clock the rising sun turned their white masses to a burnished copper colour; by contrast the Montalban Ridge was a dismal, wet, gloomy patch of dead forest. At last the sun reddened the top of the ridge and creeping gradually down the slope kindled the woods as it progressed and shone merrily between the logs of the camp. Still shivering, we emerged from our blankets and walked behind the camp where the sun was warm. If nature ever seems inanimate it is not on such a morning as this. The clouds and the trees were in motion. The sun sparkled on bright rocks on Rocky Branch ridge. At the

end of the long valley Pequaket stood sharp and clear, rosy with light. Not a suspicion of haze coloured the air. Our breath steamed as on a winter's day. Indeed, the world never seemed fresher or more real. We flung our blankets over the roof to dry; and while we warmed ourselves at the fire and over a pot of hot coffee, we wondered how low the clouds hung on Mt. Washington. Would there be a view? Or would a storm on the summit make climbing foolhardy?

When Rastignac beheld for the first time the towers of Paris he shook his fist and exclaimed, "*A nous deux, maintenant!*" It was a defiance well in keeping with his career. Before the granite towers of Mt. Washington, however, we did not simmer with defiance, perhaps because the conquest would be less a matter of wit than of strength in which the advantage was scarcely with us. On this day, if all went well, we should stand on the top of New England; we should look down on summits which in themselves had seemed sufficiently difficult during the past eight days.

"I had reached the end of my journey," wrote Jacques Balmat of his impression on reaching the summit of Mont Blanc. "I had come to a place where no one—where neither the eagle nor the chamois—had ever been before me. I had got there alone, without other help than that of my own will. Everything that surrounded me seemed to be my own property. I was the King of Mont Blanc—the statue of this tremendous pedestal." Ah, that was a mountain indeed, and a moment, too—a first climb—when the writer may well aspire to rhetorical grandiloquence and shoot words into the literary air madly. But we should have our little thrill also on Mt. Washington in the humble Appalachian Range. Emotion is not reckoned in numbers of feet. The top of a mountain anywhere brings the same satisfaction. "In every landscape," Emerson wrote, "the point of astonishment is the meeting of the sky and earth, and that is seen from the first hillock as well as from the top of the Alleghenies."

Pierre: I beg your pardon, but have you ever climbed Mt. Blanc?

The Author: Why no, not exactly.

Pierre: Not exactly! What do you mean? Have you been on the top of Mont Blanc, or have you not? Answer yes or no.

The Author: No, I have never been on the top of Mont Blanc —not exactly.

Pierre: Merciful Providence! Stop this bastardly qualification. If you have never been on the summit of Mont Blanc, it is clear to me that you have never been on the summit of Mont Blanc. "Not exactly!" What do you mean?

The Author: Why, I mean, old fellow, I have never been on the summit of Mont Blanc, but I have been on the summits of Chocorua and Whiteface and Passaconaway, and for that matter on the summit of the Görnergrat three times, and practically on the summit of the Matterhorn. A few feet more or less makes little difference.

Pierre: To a dull person like myself the difference between being on the summit of Mont Blanc and not being exactly on the summit of Mont Blanc is nothing more nor less than the difference between being on the summit of Mont Blanc and not being on the summit of Mont Blanc. All else is hypocrisy and pretence—or literature, which is much the same thing. A certain Dr. Cook once got into trouble because he said he climbed to the top of Mt. McKinley, although he didn't; that is, not exactly. Well, it turns out that he was not much of an explorer, but still a fust-class lit'ry feller.

*   *   *

We rolled up our blankets when they had been sufficiently dried and warmed by the sun, struggled into the straps of our packs, and started up the trail over the last two summits of Isolation for the first view of the Presidential Range. It was another brisk day, fine for climbing, the whole world sparkling and vibrant—that being our own mood. The trail climbed a little, twisted through a dismal, vexed patch of woods, and then thrust us on a shelf before which the mountain giants were seated in a clumsy circle. One does not burst in upon their council with complete equanimity; here the rhythms of life move at a higher pitch, and mere humans must readjust themselves, wriggle out of their puny selves, cast off the slough of workaday existence, reorient themselves, take new bearings and prepare for bigger things. It is a large order. We dropped the packs and strained to add a cubit to our stature; there is room enough above for expansion.

To the north, and at our feet, a ravine fell away sharply to the bed of a river; beyond that the Presidentials rose to loftier heights where wind, weather, cloud and bare summits created another world. It was, indeed, a magnificent spectacle of green, unbending forest, sharp rocks, an occasional foaming cascade, and hurrying cloud. The lines from valley to peak and from peak to peak were on a vast scale, daring achievements of super-artistry, the gestures of a dazzling imagination. Clinton, the lowest of the range, was clear. Boott Spur was alternately clear and murky. But Washington, Monroe, Franklin and Pleasant were hidden in the clouds whither the curious must climb to see them. We ran down to the valley and started up the Boott Spur trail more discreetly, gradually leaving the thick forest and emerging into wind, cold from the clouds and summits. On the first bit of exposed ridge the wind was a gale. We took shelter long enough to put on the extra woollen shirts and to tie our hats with cord to the packs; then on once more against the buffeting gale which blew us out of the trail at times and played rude pranks with the human centre of gravity. Now and then we sought shelter behind the huge boulders which sprinkle the Boott Spur mountain side, and smoked at ease while the wind whistled at our backs. Not a vestige of haze tempered the horizon; the view was tremendous in scope, everything clear, one of the wonders which occur in the mountains, but rarely. Like the Presidentials, the Franconia mountains were mostly in cloud. But just south of them Camel's Hump was clear, many miles away in Vermont; and the vast stretch of far country south of the Sandwich Range and the Ossipees was graphic in detail. As we climbed higher, Carter Dome worked clear of cloud. To the west the peaks of Pleasant, Franklin and Monroe blew clear; only the lofty cone of Washington was now hidden. And as we approached the tip of Boott Spur (5,520 feet), Washington appeared, first with alternating snatches of visibility and flying cloud, at last completely free. Only 700 feet above Boott Spur and less than a mile away as the crow flies were the Summit House, the queer little cars of the Mt. Washington Railroad, and a black throng of tourists. It was a shock to see so many of them and to know that most had come by train or motor car, by the same agencies, in fine, by which they pass through the world all their days. So this was not another world after all, not the home of the gods, nor of giants either; but the stopping-place of a titillated mob, the chance for a new thrill, purchased like all thrills, with specie.

THE summit was an hour's climb from the crest of Boott Spur where we were standing and gazing. It would be no arduous task to climb those few hundred feet to the top of New England and no unprecedented venture then to imagine ourselves "the statues of this tremendous pedestal." But our ardour had now cooled; the whole promenade was endangered by aliens, by barbarians from a strange land. Down behind the summit crags we were protected from the wind and warmed by the sun. We munched chocolate and smoked leisurely. Higher than any of the mountains to the south and east, we could look over the Carter-Moriah Range, over Baldface and Sable; perhaps the flat, blue area most distant in the south-east was Portland Harbour, which is said to be visible from Washington on clear days. How many mountains, hills, ponds, roads, villages can be seen from Boott Spur on a clear day? What a wealth of natural beauty! And yet how large a place does it hold, not in the world, but in the whole universe? The variety of colours ran from the greenish blue, or perhaps blueish green, of Carter to the pure blue of the most distant hills. By some sort of optical illusion every range seemed outlined with a dark-blue line. And the cloud effects were extraordinary in variety, in pageantry, sending a procession of shadows and sunlit spots across Carter. According to their distances away, the different parades seemed to move at different speeds. Those overhead swept by at express-train speed; those farthest away were almost still. It was all extraordinarily beautiful, too much so, almost—more than we could assimilate and hold; and an indica-

From a painting by G. N. Frankenstein.

J. H. Bufford & Co. Lith. Boston.

MOUNT WASHINGTON, OVER TUCKERMAN'S RAVINE.

Oakes' White Mountain Scenery., Plate 16

Entered according to act of Congress in the year 1848 by W. Oakes, in the Clerks office of the District Court of Mass.

tion of how much mystery behind it, what divine or pagan forces? "What can be expressed in words," said Thoreau, "can be expressed in life." The converse is never true.

We were far too comfortable to move; a warm lethargy crept over us agreeably. Pierre dipped into his pack for Socrates and began to read at random. As chance would have it he hit on a dialogue between Socrates and Euthydemus on the definition of beauty. "And can we define the beautiful in any other way than if you term whatever is beautiful—whether a person, or a vase, or anything else whatsoever—beautiful for whatever purpose you know that it is beautiful?" asked Socrates with confusing simplicity. "No, indeed," said Euthydemus, the simple-minded. "For whatever purpose, then, anything may be useful, for that purpose it is beautiful to use it?" "Certainly." "And is anything beautiful for any other purpose than that for which it is beautiful to use it?" "For no other purpose," Euthydemus replied. "What is useful is beautiful, therefore, for that purpose for which it is useful?" "So I think," said he, no doubt in a vigorous tone of finality.

Then we fell to discussing the beauty of forests and mountains, but in truth we could not apply Socrates' definition with much satisfaction. If beauty consists in usefulness, one must determine for what uses these mountains and forests are best suited. And of what use are they, save as grist for the lumberman? What of the mountains after they have been stripped of their timber? Are they still beautiful, or has their beauty vanished? Perhaps Socrates, who lived in a country whose natural beauty is by no means insignificant, would not be stumped to reconcile natural beauty with his all-embracing test of usefulness on the score of spiritual values. However, we were reminded that all his followers did not agree with his proffers of wisdom. For when at the banquet Socrates had contended that his features were the most beautiful in the room because the most useful—his flat nose with wide, upturned nostrils being especially well formed for smelling, and his thick and large lips giving his kisses an especially fine quality of sweetness and lusciousness—the company all voted against him. In the prospect from Boott Spur we could see no beauty easily adaptable to Socrates' definition. Perhaps Socrates was wrong; perhaps the fulminating Théophile Gautier was more nearly right in the preface to "Mademoiselle de Maupin": "There is nothing truly beautiful but that which can never be of any use whatsoever; everything useful is ugly, for it is the expression of some need, and man's needs are ignoble and disgusting like his own poor and infirm nature. The most useful place in a house is the water-closet."

We should have enjoyed lingering on such a vantage-point as the sheltered crest of Boott Spur, monarchs in our own right of a vast domain; but several mundane affairs of life urged us on. The store of food had been dwindling in an alarming fashion; we had no more oatmeal, pancake-flour, coffee, baked beans, bacon or sugar. In Pinkham Notch at the foot of the mountain we knew of a camp where all such things might be had; and towards noon we began picking a way cautiously down the pre-

cipitous southern face of Boott Spur, over loose and treacherous rocks which have tumbled from the summit of the ridge. It was an exhilarating place, Tuckerman Ravine falling away at a rapid angle on the left, the majestic cone of Washington flung skywards beyond. From the tree-line the Boott Spur trail slips into Tuckerman Ravine with a sheer grade which makes descending a sport and climbing a sore achievement. Soon we left the parapets far above and swung rapidly towards the river, checking speed by clutching the trees along the way. We were almost down when we heard voices—the first human sounds in three days. It is said that when Livingstone was found in Africa he did not rejoice at the prospect of returning to civilization. After three days on the Montalban Ridge neither were we prepared to simmer down again to the tepid warmth of "good society," to descend from self-imposed adventure to the ignoble level of touring. The voices were those of three climbers who were hurrying to the summit via Boott Spur in order to be down again before evening. They had come by automobile that morning from Lake Winnepesaukee, whither they must return the same day. The commuter's life is a prolonged abortion.

We kept on down the trail, across the river and up a few rods towards Tuckerman Ravine to a U.S. Forest Reserve shelter near Hermit Lake. Another party of campers had left their equipment there, but without knowing their number we decided that two more would not cramp the sleeping-space, however much it might cramp our insolent style. After luncheon we emptied one pack and set out down the trail to Pinkham Notch for provisions, two miles below. Free of the packs, we raced along at a good pace and passed several groups of tourists who had come down from the summit and who not unreasonably resented our speed. But judging by our usual pace we had little time to spare if we were to be back in camp before nightfall, and we had a real respect for climbing back with a full load. The Pinkham Notch lodge supplied us with all the food we needed; the empty pack was now quite full and heavy. In climbing up the mountain to camp the plan was for each man to carry the pack ten minutes by the watch and then climb unburdened ten minutes more while his companion strained under the shoulder straps. And we would climb as briskly as possible until we were exhausted; then rest and get under way once more. But how absurdly we had underestimated our strength. We tore up the trail rapidly, passing again most of those whom we had passed coming down, and were back in camp in forty minutes with evening still almost two hours away. There was a keen satisfaction about all that, but an entirely false economy. Abstract temperance is in no wise a virtue; temperance in speed, however, is the high wisdom of human life.

The other campers were three young lads from Salem who had never been in the woods or mountains before. They had read of the joys and freedoms of camping-life and had come north to embrace them ardently. Alas! they were ill-prepared by equipment and experience, had difficulty in building fires, insisted upon undressing when they went to bed and as a result

I suppose that the connoisseurs and the gourmands of forest pleasures would give the first place in the catalogue of its delights to the silence of its deepest fastnesses. . . . But I plead for the voice of the waters. There is something in the sound of a mountain brook—at least so long as it does not swell to the hoarseness of a torrent—which breaks the forest silences only to accentuate them, and falls upon the ear with a touch like that of a leaf as it drops upon the forest floor.

—JOHN COLEMAN ADAMS

shivered the cold night through. Their low shoes, skull-caps and blazing neckties gave them a gay appearance which belied the success of their adventure. The potatoes they carried made their packs unbearably heavy; the sardines and canned clam chowder proved monotonous diet, while the eggs were no more satisfying. We ventured ironically that "camping is a great life," to which they assented in unison—laconically. After supper they crept into a warm corner of the camp, played cards, and sang popular songs in what is known as "close harmony," much practised on soft spring evenings on college campuses in America. The night grew chilly as the cold air on the Mt. Washington summit slipped down to the floor of the Ravine. We took off our boots but put on all the clothes we had, buttoned up tightly and rolled inside our blankets. The Salem adventurers undressed, obedient to arbitrary rules of hygiene and sanitation. They shivered as the night grew chilly. Our barbarous night-clothing kept us unclean and thoroughly comfortable. Camping in the mountains and strolling by day near the city are not to be confused so lightly.

DURING the night the temperature went down, but not so low as when we spent a huddled and uncomfortable night at Camp Isolation. And Hermit Lake was sheltered from the wind, which still kept up a rumbling monotone, by the crags which encircle Tuckerman Ravine from Lion Head to Boott Spur. By morning the back of the gale had been broken. When we emerged from the camp on Tuesday morning to make the first yawning observations of sky and weather, a bank of cirro-stratus clouds shut off the empyrean, and like a blanket had kept the natural heat from rising from the earth. The temperature was more agreeable, but even Pierre predicted rain; accordingly we all felt that there was little hope.

We climbed a ledge for a broader sweep towards the east. Clouds covered the whole sky in that significant direction. Once the sun worked through and shone brightly, boiling pure gold indeed. The outlook for good weather, however, was not promising; we considered remaining in camp all day. But Tuckerman Ravine is far too popular a place for seclusion, and besides we were eager to cross two huge ridges of Washington and descend into the Great Gulf beyond, where a camp and a towering cirque of mountains give life in the forest a fresh and singular grace. The beauty of that wild chasm is worth a little wetting. By 9:30 we were through breakfast and on the trail through Tuckerman Ravine.

The Ravine was fairly crowded with tourists on their way to the top of Mt. Washington. Sunday and Monday had been the sort of fine "mountain weather" which inevitably draws climbers to the peaks in great numbers. Some of them, however, inevitably delay, undecided whether to climb or to remain on level ground, and like the foolish virgins find their equipment incomplete when they need it most. Accordingly, they arrive too late for the ceremonies. Many of those whom we passed in the Ravine had thus been stirred out of their homes one day too late, and a brief shower which came dancing down from the cone reminded them somewhat lugubriously of their fatal sluggishness.

It was good to be under way again. Ahead rose the steep wall of Tuckerman Ravine, rocky and fairly barren, yet whitened here and there by innumerable little waterfalls. Beside the trail Cutler River roared so loudly that human voices could not carry across. At one turning where the trail crosses the river we saw no place where, encumbered by packs, we could get to the other shore without wading. While I was exploring the river-bank, Pierre discovered the weakness in this little barrier, and leaped to the other side. He shouted directions at the top of his voice, but the roar of swift water was all I could hear. Sign-language alone was intelligible. Our packs were again heavy with a full quota of provisions, and the memory of previous climbs in Tuckerman Ravine served to warn us that we had a morning of hard work in prospect. It is said, generally from the depths of an easy-chair, that people thrive on difficulties. By this time, however, we knew that we throve quite as well on languorous ease; and were willing to leave steep climbing to those who find pleasure in it. Yet our muscles were now so toughened after nine days in the mountains that we clambered up the headwall steadily without resting and were not even breathless when we came to the top. Here we left the other climbers with whom we had been chatting pleasantly all the way, and turned off on the Six Husbands Trail through the Alpine Garden.

IT WAS a soft, summery day. The sting was gone from the air; the wind was no longer biting. After more than two days of vigorous weather, haze was stealing back into the mountains, taming the wildness of the view and shortening its sweep. It was difficult to believe that we were in the New England highlands, more than 5,000 feet above sea level. We walked on slowly, chatting and frittering away the morning; and at the head of Huntington Ravine we sat down on a shelf of rock and took our ease, overlooking a rugged and pathless chimney up Mt. Washington. A bumble-bee, symbol of hot fields, buzzed around lazily. All about us were miniature blueberry-bushes, an inch and a half in height, each one supporting a sour, unripened berry. The most conspicuous flower was the mountain sandwort. The houstonia, an early spring flower on the lowlands, was scarcely less numerous. In a nearby grassy plain the rank Indian poke and the American star flower grew abundantly. There were also pyrola and bluebells. Noon approached and passed before we got under way again, over a blackened ridge of jagged rock.

Over that ridge we were beyond the height of land for the day and well on the way to the Great Gulf, most interesting of all corners of the White Mountains. Beyond this great chasm the northern peaks came into view—Clay, Jefferson, Adams and Madison, nobler summits than those which rise to the south of Mt. Washington. We admired their bold contours; but our immediate concern was the Great Gulf which fell away at our feet. Here the Six Husbands Trail drops 2,000 feet in the space of one mile, and the view from the top is a dizzy one. The heavy, forested floor so far below appears as a rough field, covered with stubble. And the roar of Peabody River at the bottom is for ever echoing from the crags on three sides, humming and buzzing all day and night from a wild and crooked gorge, al-

ready worn deep, yet deeper every day. For five varied miles Peabody River drains these mountain ridges, whirls in pot-holes, foams over falls, and in the spring grinds heavy boulders along its bed.

We prepared for a strenuous descent. The Six Husbands Trail, it is said, was named in honour of Weetamoo, an Indian queen, whose vitality wore out six husbands. Well and boldly named; we could not have been in her service long. For down we went, rapidly, always alert to rolling stones and unfortunate slides, checking our descent by clutching at rocks and the branches of trees, amid a veritable bastinado. The trees proved to be the stoutest and yet the most pliable brakes, and we made constant use of them, grasping a spruce branch at the top of a slide, slipping down in a rush, releasing the first branch and clutching another until we were safely at the bottom. By three o'clock we were on the floor of the Gulf and on the trail to camp. The mountain summits were smoking with cloud; soon the rain, anticipated since morning, began to come down gently.

Well, we were prepared for the rain, and with shelter close at hand, could manage to enjoy it, notwithstanding the difficulties it puts in the way of camp-cooking. But we were not prepared to find two men and two women in camp who treated us like social outcasts and indicated that even here in the wilderness the use of the only shelter, provided for all comers, was somewhat in the nature of a concession on their part. Of course we did not make a distinguished appearance. A week and more of travel had soiled and torn our clothing, had scarred our boots; and our faces, otherwise clean, were black with beards several days old. One would not enter a drawing-room in that fashion. But so long as one has strength enough to enter a mountain shelter, and modesty enough to keep reasonably silent, one's appearance may well be passed over. We resented the air of charity with which these people made a little room for us, and the hostility with which they regarded us, responding in bored monosyllables to our innocuous efforts at conversation. Nevertheless, we cooked luncheon and ate it under shelter while the rain pattered on the roof. Our neighbours "put on a little dog" to impress us, or so we concluded; chattered in a superior manner about the society in which they moved at home and about the hotel where they were summer guests. We sat in camp meekly enough, hoping to be admitted to the conversation; but we were ignored completely, and to break the spell if possible, we went out into the woods in search of a dry tree to chop up for fire-wood. Even this contribution to mutual comfort did not put us on the social register of the Great Gulf. For the rest of the day we languished inoffensively inside the camp, wondering vaguely if, after all, socialism might not be the panacea for a warped and tyrannical civilization. Our neighbours were still talking of dances, bridge parties, college class-day functions, and were gossiping about their sophisticated friends when we fell asleep that night with the noise of Peabody River in our ears. It is amazing how we hold fast to the tawdry business of the city when we wander into the woods. After two years and two months on the shores of Walden Pond, Thoreau left the woods because, as he said, "It seemed to me that I had more lives to live, and could not spare any more time for that one." Most of us live more brittle lives than that.

How begrudgingly we let new impressions sink in. The woods ring with bird-songs and are redolent of the sweet odours of trees and flowers. But the summer guests knit on the hotel veranda, play cards and take genteel walks along the edge of the woods, meanwhile dressed as carefully as though happiness depended upon circumspect appearance. Even when we penetrate to the heart of the mountains and complain of the weight of our packs, we insist upon carrying the world with us as a gratuitous burden.

After breakfast on Wednesday our camp-mates turned towards home. As they disappeared through the trees we did a song and dance about camp, brandishing the ax and the frying-pan. The Great Gulf was for the time being our own; there was no one in camp to exchange significant glances over whatever we chose to do or say. We decided first to discover what sort of place we were in —what were its beauties and its peculiar advantages. The Gulf is as impressive a place from the bottom as from the surrounding peaks. To the east the Gothic rim of the forest frets the sky. Everywhere else mountains crowd the horizon, so close that their jagged ridges seem almost overhead. Behind a fringe of woods Peabody River rushes over its turbulent bed a few hundred yards from the camp. Its voice was a steady roar, accompanied by more distinct, finer-articulated, higher-pitched side remarks which more than once by their human quality deceived us into expecting a procession of other campers down the trail. We lazed about in the sunshine, splitting wood enough to last through the next morning, watching the crossbills and pine grosbeaks which flitted about the fireplace, and letting the varied effects of this magnificent chasm sink into our minds. One cannot sit in the doorway of that camp without gazing at the knee of Jefferson which looms so high on the left. True symbol of the Great Gulf, it serves as a gauge against which everything else may be measured. A few rods upstream we found a noisy, flashing pool of Peabody River in the confusion of boulders, rapids and miniature falls—the knee of Jefferson clearing the tree tops on the western side. The water was too cold for languid bathing. He who bathes in mountain streams must be no more sluggish than they. We plunged in, leaped out again instantly, soaped ourselves, and plunged again. It was invigorating sport. Rubbed dry to a tingle of warmth we washed our clothes again—soaped them on the flat rocks, rinsed them in the swift water which tugged at them gently. Once Pierre let a sock float out of his grasp; he jumped after it, but it was soon tumbling over little falls mockingly and sailing swiftly across pools and hurrying out of sight round a curve in the stream. In the afternoon we strolled upstream to a series of pulsating falls. There for several hundred feet Peabody River tumbles over a succession of transverse ledges and spills at length into a dark pool where the white fury of the water cools into sudden tranquillity, and where the steady, shrill cry of foaming water sinks to a muffled gurgling. We worked our way down river, casting trout flies across the darkest pools. The iridescent fish did not respond, but the variety of the river, the pot-holes, the ledges worn smooth, the logs cast up securely on the banks, the boulders lodged tightly around the pools, were quite as fascinating and told quite as much of the river.

I never merited this grace, that when I face upstream I scent the virgin breath of mountains, I feel a spray of mist on my cheeks and lips, I hear a ceaseless splash and susurrus, a sound of water not merely poured smoothly down air to fill a steady pool, but tumbling live about, over, under, around, between, through an intricate speckling of rock. . . . I never merited this grace, that when I face upstream I see the light on the water careening towards me, inevitably, freely, down a graded series of terraces like the balanced winged platforms on an infiite inexhaustible font. "Ho, if you are thirsty, come down to the water; ho, if you are hungry, come and sit and eat." This is the present, at last. . . . This is the now, this flickering, broken light, this air that the wind of the future presses down my throat, pumping me buoyant and giddy with praise.

—ANNIE DILLARD

MAD RIVER

WHY dost thou wildly rush and roar,
　　Mad River, O Mad River?
Wilt thou not pause and cease to pour
Thy hurrying, headlong waters o'er
　　This rocky shelf forever?

What secret trouble stirs thy breast?
　　Why all this fret and flurry?
Dost thou not know that what is best
In this too restless world is rest
　　From over-work and worry?

THE RIVER

What wouldst thou in these mountains seek,
　　O stranger from the city?
Is it perhaps some foolish freak
Of thine, to put the words I speak
　　Into a plaintive ditty?

TRAVELLER

Yes; I would learn of thee thy song,
　　With all its flowing numbers,
And in a voice as fresh and strong
As thine is, sing it all day long,
　　And hear it in my slumbers.

THE RIVER

A brooklet nameless and unknown
　　Was I at first, resembling
A little child, that all alone
Comes venturing down the stairs of stone,
　　Irresolute and trembling.

Later, by wayward fancies led,
　　For the wide world I panted;
Out of the forest, dark and dread,
Across the open fields I fled,
　　Like one pursued and haunted.

I tossed my arms, I sang aloud,
　　My voice exultant blending
With thunder from the passing cloud,
The wind, the forest bent and bowed,
　　The rush of rain descending.

I heard the distant ocean call,
　　Imploring and entreating;
Drawn onward, o'er this rocky wall
I plunged, and the loud waterfall
　　Made answer to the greeting.

And now, beset with many ills,
　　A toilsome life I follow;
Compelled to carry from the hills
These logs to the impatient mills
　　Below there in the hollow.

Yet something ever cheers and charms
　　The rudeness of my labors;
Daily I water with these arms
The cattle of a hundred farms,
　　And have the birds for neighbors.

Men call me Mad, and well they may,
　　When, full of rage and trouble,
I burst my banks of sand and clay,
And sweep their wooden bridge away,
　　Like withered reeds or stubble.

Now go and write thy little rhyme,
　　As of thine own creating.
Thou seest the day is past its prime;
I can no longer waste my time;
　　The mills are tired of waiting.

—HENRY WADSWORTH LONGFELLOW

The Author: Every one talks of the heart of the mountains. That term is sufficiently ambiguous to sustain a dunghill of buncombe. Nevertheless, I say Peabody River is the heart of the Great Gulf.

Pierre: You speak for yourself. Call Peabody River the heart of the Great Gulf if you wish, but don't draw me into silly controversies.

The Author: Come now, don't stoop to personalities. Either Peabody River is or is not the heart of the Great Gulf. If it is, admit it; if not, why not? Don't let your middleclass prejudices creep out in this fashion, and don't be an intellectual bounder.

Pierre: You talk like a schoolmaster. Well, granting that Peabody River is the heart of the Great Gulf, the burden of the proof is upon you.

The Author: To be sure it is. The proof is easy enough. The heart is the seat of the affections, the inmost or essential part, the spirit. Therefore, Peabody River is the heart of the Great Gulf.

Pierre: Stop, in the name of St. Denis! Nothing, by Jupiter, is clear according to this way of reasoning. That is equivalent to saying, "The pterodactyl is an extinct bird. Therefore, all extinct birds are pterodactyls." Don't talk like a blooming Auk.

The Author: Oh, I can complete the argument if I must. I thought you were clever enough to fill in what I did not supply.

Pierre: Yes, you hoped I would make the argument for you.

The Author: Nothing of the kind. Let me get in a word edgewise, will you? Confound it—less heat and more light. Now listen. What are the qualities of the Great Gulf's spirit? They are purity, strength, breadth, constant activity, wildness, determination, indifference to obstacles. The Peabody River, which flows through the centre of the Great Gulf and whose little tributaries spill from the summits of the mountains, feeling the steepness of these slopes, has also those abstract qualities of the Gulf. Therefore, the Peabody River is the heart of the Great Gulf.

Pierre: The heart of Timbuctoo! A pathetic fallacy, or I'm the Delphic oracle. You frame the first part of your argument to prove the last part. You have no reverence for the whole truth. You talk like a senator amending the tariff bill.

The Author: You have no feeling for beauty.

Pierre: Your feeling for beauty is your own pompous egotism.

The Author: You're a conceited and sullen blockhead.

*   *   *

At last we turned back towards the camp, wondering how many others had come there in our absence. The camp was empty. At least for the present we were free. We took our clothes in from the line, where they were fastened with birch twigs split like clothes-pins, and read with much relish Socrates' pleasantries during a visit to Theodota, the popular Athenian courtesan; and his dry reasoning with Euthydemus when that complacent young man proposed publicly to accuse his father of the murder of a servant. Meanwhile, Peabody River played us for gulls, ventriloquizing and chattering like belated campers on the trail. Several times one or the other of us said, "Here comes some one"; but although we stopped talking and looked down the trail, no one came. When the sun fell behind Jefferson and night crept down the headwall of the Gulf we were still monarchs of this secluded shelter. After supper a bank of stratus clouds moved across the sky, exquisitely formed like fine sand ripples on the sea-shore. We had a brisk campfire that night, built of several big logs, which are numerous in that forest. The flames were still leaping and filling the camp with ruddy light and dancing shadows when we rolled up in our blankets.

In the night I dreamed of trout-fishing; and, when at length I awoke, it seemed a fable that this painted fish swam there so near my couch, and rose to our hooks the last evening, and I doubted if I had not dreamed it all. So I arose before dawn to test its truth, while my companions were still sleeping. There stood Ktaadn with distinct and cloudless outline in the moonlight; and the rippling of the rapids was the only sound to break the stillness. Standing on the shore, I once more cast my line into the stream, and found the dream to be real and the fable true. The speckled trout and silvery roach, like flying-fish, sped swiftly through the moonlight air, describing bright arcs on the dark side of Ktaadn, until moonlight, now facing into daylight, brought satiety to my mind, and the minds of my companions, who had joined me.

—HENRY DAVID THOREAU

NIGHT comes early and dawn comes late in Great Gulf. We were up on Thursday morning long before the sun spilled over Chandler Ridge and warmed this deep canyon where the chill of night lingers far into the day. We were up early, earlier than on any day previous, for an arduous journey was ahead of us in uncertain weather. We had scrambled into the Gulf on Tuesday with some physical effort; that would be as nothing, however, in comparison with the effort required to get out again, to scale the steep ridges of Mt. Washington and so get under way for Mizpah Spring Camp on Mt. Clinton. Before retiring on Wednesday evening we had consulted the map most earnestly; we had followed the course of all trails up from the Gulf—up Jefferson, up Clay, up Washington from Hermit Lake, and up the Six Husbands Trail by which we had come in. Was it possible that all the paths climbed precipitous ridges? Was there no easy course for the lackadaisical climber? Alas! we had come to an impasse; and, except towards the Glen House, where no real mountaineer can bear to go, we must climb with our hands as well as our feet to leave this forested valley, and so we had concluded to storm the Six Husbands Trail again as the easiest route to Mt. Clinton. A certain French king of childhood myth is said to have marched his men right up a hill and marched them back again. And so the innocent myths of childhood became the realities of mature old age. We surveyed the high ridges behind camp with a patient but weary eye and hoped that the good God would bless our labours upward. Even to the most self-sufficient there comes a day when human powers are in themselves too weak for necessary achievements.

It seemed a sacrilege to be astir so long before the rising of the sun. Scraggles of white mist floated like ghosts about the summit of Jefferson; the air was cold and moist; the rough stone hearth, where merry fires had been dancing ten hours ago, was wet with dew and dead; the woods were filled with night. While nature sleeps, man ought to sleep as well. Shivering with cold, we set about kindling a fire mechanically, without enthusiasm, still half-asleep, as though we had been imposed upon. It was a phlegmatic procedure. Among the refinements of Great Gulf Camp is a table of rough slabs nailed to tree-stumps, with benches nailed on either side of similar material. Well, it is rough, to be sure; but few urban restaurants are half as picturesque. When we had breakfast smoking on that table and sat down to this mountain-girdled meal, we blessed the good fortune which had put all this rugged beauty at our personal disposition and cursed the stupid impulse which set us on the trail again in search of other places. It is hard to kill the instinct which moves us on to new adventures. Some people call that instinct progress. And for proof they point unimaginatively to the modern world about them.

Pierre: Look here, stop moralizing, in heaven's name! The facts of this journey and its impressions are quite sufficient. Holy smoke, why argue about them! I no sooner get interested in this record than a dash of moralizing affects me like an emetic.

The Author: Come, come! Temper thy speech, my friend. Moralizing is no more disgusting, I'm sure, than such coarse language.

Pierre: That may be true, but consider the provocation. You can't poke animals forever without expecting them to snarl. I'll put up with almost any amount of virtue in this book, but I'm damned if I'll put up with morality.

*   *   *

The dishes were washed and the packs were ready by half past seven. We smoked a last pipe leisurely in the doorway, then swung the packs on our shoulders and started down the trail. The sun had come out for a brief interval but now hid behind the clouds.

The eerie voices of Peabody River had been in our ears now for thirty-six hours, singing occult music to which we responded but which we could scarcely understand. For a few rods the Six Husbands Trail follows the river closely, through chambers of varying music, and then turns away at a right angle. We plodded on slowly, over soft, cushionlike moss, under trees whose bark was velvety with moss, towards the flank of Mt. Washington, always farther away from the river, whose voice grew constantly dimmer. Then up we went at a breathless scramble, leaning against the trees to recover lost wind, and up once more with gritted teeth. Almost before we realized it, we were high above the floor of Great Gulf. And now the roar of Peabody River came loud again, a siren cry beseeching us to turn round and come back again. God knows it was hard enough to go on without that haunting entreaty. By nine o'clock we had climbed the 2,000 feet to the parapet, and still the noise of Peabody River echoed in our ears.

Black clouds were tearing across the summits of Clay, Jefferson and Adams, gradually turning to white, floating up buoyantly and leaving the peaks clear. Some fragments drifted across the Great Gulf where new currents of air tore them apart and blew them high above the summits. We were treated also with mountain echoes, created by blasting on the carriage-road. The voices of Clay, Jefferson and Adams were speaking in quick succession. We timed them. The first eight seconds after the blasts were soundless. Then echoes began on Clay and thundered round the bow of the Great Gulf for seventeen seconds—twenty-five seconds in all from report to last echo.

The clouds were heavy over the cone of Mt. Washington, and as we climbed up the ridge towards the Alpine Garden we were

soon engulfed in them. They were forming on the headwall of Huntington Ravine where a damp south-east wind was cooled and condensed on the cold rocks of the mountain. Objects thirty feet away were invisible. And our progress from cairn to cairn was curiously uncertain and mysterious, and sometimes almost an adventure. Sometimes the fog blew away momentarily, clearing to the tip of the mountain, a thousand feet above. Such moments were reassuring, for we knew that we were still on the right trail. Then, the mist settling down heavy again, we were alone in an unknown land. Thus for a half-hour we plodded across the murky Alpine Garden until we heard the roar of a mountain torrent ahead and below. It was Cutler River, foaming down the headwall of Tuckerman Ravine. While we rested on the crest of that ridge the clouds rolled up in ponderous masses, uncovering the floor of the Ravine until Hermit Lake was visible; and finally Pinkham Notch and Wildcat Mountain, veiled with the most translucent blue possible. But the view was soon cut off. By noon-time the clouds were dense once more. We took our bearings by compass and map, and set out across Bigelow Lawn to the Crawford Path. Somewhere on that trail was a spring where we hoped to cook lunch, and we hurried on in search of it.

MAN'S presence on mountain summits, as Thoreau explained, and as this apostolic book has constantly repeated, is always a slight insult to the gods; and on cloudy days when fog tears over the summits it is the basest sort of intrusion, indulged in only by prying busybodies who peep in upon things intended for nobler eyes. Occasionally, even on Mt. Washington, the gods seek vengeance; then the intruders never return to the walks of man. As we twisted on through the columns of damp crags, like giants with their heads in the cloud, and pushed into the wet gale sweeping up from Oakes Gulf with its panoply of mist, we knew ourselves to be intruders—intruders on a day of superhuman toil, when the gods were concerned exclusively with their own business; and we knew that we must make shift for ourselves like the chance spectator at a theatrical rehearsal, whose chief concern is to keep out of the way. To walk the exposed ridges on such a roaring day is an experience; it is not, however, a pleasure.

Suddenly rain beat into our faces. We dropped the packs, pulled out the ponchos, and in the gale pulled them over our heads while they flapped angrily, and the ends struggled not to be caught. With much difficulty, and with the rain stinging his face and hands, Pierre managed to tie mine in place; and then I performed the same service for him. By this time the storm was fairly upon us, hissing on the wet rocks, spattering and singing in the pools, blowing up aggressively under our hats, rattling on the hard surface of the ponchos—a mad whirl and scurry of rebellious elements. The mountain ridges took the storm patiently, well used to this fury and more, streaming with rain; and the little spruce-trees which grew wherever they had footing bent before the gusts of wind, "writhed and reached and feared the rain."

Lunch-hour came while we still had several miles to walk on the exposed Crawford Path, under the summits of Monroe and Pleasant which were battling with the storm above, where we could not see them; but although we were hungry we hurried on, eager only to reach shelter as soon as possible. A sign marking the bypath to the summit of Mt. Pleasant was our first indication of distance covered; we took new heart and pushed on through the fog. At last the summit-cairn of Mt. Clinton loomed up, as serene as a lighthouse in a rolling sea. Here we might leave the Crawford Path and drop down into the woods, and into a less truculent world, like a ship's cabin while a storm roars outside. The trees were dripping, and the black forest muck was ankle-deep and slippery. We sloshed down the mountain ponderously, through trees and fog, slipping and sliding, to Mizpah Spring Camp. Hats and ponchos were dripping, leggings were damp, and boots were muddy; but except for wet knees we were dry and warm and were glad to be out of the blustering sky-line storm.

If I wished to see a mountain or other scenery under the most favorable auspices, I would go to it in foul weather, so as to be there when it cleared up; we are then in the most suitable mood, and nature is most fresh and inspiring. There is no serenity so fair as that which is just established in a tearful eye.

—HENRY DAVID THOREAU

FRAGMENTARY BLUE

Why make so much of fragmentary blue
In here and there a bird, or butterfly,
In flower, or wearing-stone, or open eye,
When heaven presents in sheets the solid hue?

Since earth is earth, perhaps, not heaven (as yet)—
Though some savants make earth include the sky;
And blue so far above us comes so high,
It only gives our wish for blue a whet.
                              —ROBERT FROST

The trees around camp were bright with glassy drops of rain, and the fog, writhing and lapping, softened the outlines of the forest. A young married couple had reached camp before us and was presiding over its destinies with kindly importance. We did not like to pry into their household secrets, but it was three o'clock, and the weather thick and forbidding. While they watched us with heavy eyes we went in search of a standing dead tree for fire-wood and combined luncheon and dinner in one gluttonous meal—baked beans, bacon and fried crackers, boiled rice and raisins and cocoa. And being hungry after eight hours of walking and fasting, we felt disposed to give to our eating those familiar flourishes which, by common consent, denote the not-too-civilized man's enjoyment of his food. But Pyramus and Thisbe exchanged solemn glances, while Thisbe drew up closer to Pyramus and laid her hand in his. He was *her man!* We recognized that and respected it; indeed, we felt no desire to dispute it, and considered that additional proof was superfluous. In his complaint of young married people, Lamb wrote: "They carry this preference [for each other] so undisguisedly, they perk it up into the faces of us single people so shamelessly, you cannot be in their company a moment without being made to feel, by some indirect hint or open avowal, that *you* are not the object of this preference." If that were all, one might hold one's peace. But it is infinitely more serious. One is made to feel that they represent a higher caste to which only the married are admitted, and that all others are shiftless loiterers. They are not married a month before they pretend to look with curious amusement upon all those who are still unattached. And what lengths they go, to prove themselves the sole custodians of the world's honour! Pyramus and Thisbe seemed to regard it as no more than simple justice that we should split up the wood for the camp-fire, lay the blaze at their feet and keep it burning in the rain, as black slaves look after the comfort of Oriental kings and queens. What we had considered a bit of courtesy then became a leaden duty. They spread themselves comfortably before the fire, whilst we were crowded to the corners and eked out a modicum of lonely enjoyment by smoking and listening to the patter of the rain on the roof. They thrust their secrets in our faces, referring to the various parts of their camping-equipment by fanciful names which they alone knew, and referring also to the friends of whom they talked by mysterious initials. Finally Pyramus fumbled about inside his pack and pulled out—of all things!—a ukulele; and after a bit of preliminary tuning Pyramus and Thisbe joined their voices (as marriage had joined their souls!) in husky cater-

wauling. At length, with a pitiful and melancholy air, we crept into our cold end of the camp, while Pyramus and Thisbe, sitting close together and talking in a monotone, enjoyed the warmth of our camp fire. The rain sang on the roof and dripped into little pools on the ground.

The clouds were dampening the trees near the camp when we got up early on Friday morning. Our last morning in the woods! Only yesterday, it seemed, we had entered them, clean, shaven and soft of muscle. There was no real joy in our preparations for breakfast, nor in our packing to leave the woods. By all accounts, Socrates took his cup of hemlock more cheerfully. By 7:30 we were on our way out of camp and down the three miles to Crawfords for a morning train to Boston. Our dejection was not lightened by the thought that while we were again at work in the crowded city, the successive days of rain and sunshine, the pageantry of cloud formations, and all the phenomena of the mountains would go on as serenely as usual. They were much to us while we were nothing to them. Not far from camp a spruce partridge stood alert in the trail; like all this species of the deeper woods he was not afraid to let us pass within a few feet. A hermit-thrush called languidly in the woods near the edge of the forest. In a tree near Gibbs Brook a woodpecker set up a boisterous racket—an Arctic three-toed woodpecker at last. At Passaconaway we had tried vainly to metamorphose a hairy into this rarer species. But here there was no need of such charlatanry; bird-glasses and bird-book both identified him clearly. Just then a crow cawed. We had not heard one since we left the fields at Chocorua, and his blustering note set us down into the social world as effectively as the circumspect grounds of the Crawford House a few rods beyond.

Rain began falling again before we boarded the train at Crawfords, and continued as we rumbled through the Notch. The tops of Willard, Webster and Crawford merged into the clouds so delicately that one could not see where clouds and mountains met. We smoked, gazed out of the car window, and read snatches of Socrates.

So the time passed until the train drew into Boston, and we joined the holiday throngs in the North Station. We bought the afternoon newspapers mechanically and read the headlines— "Railroad Parleys Off"; "Menace in Coal Crisis." Thus, for two weeks the same news had served its daily purpose as though newspapers chronicled progress, not apathy. So we dropped back into the same world we had left, with nothing lost and with two weeks of living on the credit side.

HILLS IN MIST

Familiar is the scene, yet strange:
    Field, roadside, tree, and stream,
Fringed with a blur of misty change,—
    The landscape of a dream!

The hills are gone; the river winds
    Under a fleecy bank:
The eye, through all its wandering, finds
    Both earth and heaven a blank.

The picture tells a tale untrue:
    Where muffling mists descend,
Where level meadows bound the view,
    The horizon does not end.

For, glimpsed beyond the spectral trees,
    Faint, penciled peaks appear;
And in this fresh, inspiring breeze
    We know the mountains near.

—LUCY LARCOM

INTO MY OWN

One of my wishes is that those dark trees,
So old and firm they scarcely show the breeze,
Were not, as 'twere, the merest mask of gloom,
But stretched away unto the edge of doom.

I should not be withheld but that some day
Into their vastness I should steal away,
Fearless of ever finding open land,
Or highway where the slow wheel pours the sand.

I do not see why I should e'er turn back,
Or those should not set forth upon my track
To overtake me, who should miss me here
And long to know if still I held them dear.

They would not find me changed from him they knew—
Only more sure of all I thought was true.
                                        —ROBERT FROST

These particles of snow which the early wind shakes down are what is stirring, or the morning news of the wood. Sometimes it is blown up above the trees, like the sand of the desert. You glance up these paths, closely imbowered by bent trees, as though the side aisles of a cathedral, and expect to hear a choir chanting from their depths. You are never so far in them as they are far before you. Their secret is where you are not and where your feet can never carry you.

—HENRY DAVID THOREAU

H. FENN.   Entered according to Act of Congress, A.D. 1872, by D. Appleton & Co. in the office of the Librarian of Congress, Washington.   S. V. HUNT

The Mount Washington Road

*Recreational development is a job
not of building roads into lovely country,
but of building receptivity
into the still unlovely human mind.*

—ALDO LEOPOLD

The AMC Hut System

THE Appalachian Mountain Club Hut System, a chain of eight mountain hostelries, extends more than fifty miles across New Hampshire's ridgelines, from Lonesome Lake near Lake Franconia Notch to Carter Notch, near the Maine border. Pinkham Notch, not exactly a hut, is the system's roadside headquarters and can comfortably hold ninety guests. Each hut is a day's hike from the next, and the last, completed in 1965, is seventy-seven years from the first.

College-aged crews who staff the system are at once cooks, custodians, and providers of trail information. They manage the huts' environs, are host to day hikers and overnighters, and perform occasional search and rescue missions. Crew members spend two or three days a week—backpacking food and supplies into the huts—tons of them.

For a hundred days running, and for a pittance, crews are exposed to tens of thousands of seekers of wildlands, and as many repetitious questions. They put in twelve hours and are on call for the remaining twelve. Yet the competition for hut jobs is fierce: three hundred applicants each year for a dozen vacancies. Among the winners over the years have been scores of collegiate athletes, several Olympians, a smattering of lawyers, fundraisers, professional skiers, Peace Corps workers, doctors, geologists, hippies, journalists, salesmen, cooks, foresters, and a pride of AMC presidents.

In 1888, twelve years after the Appalachian Mountain Club was founded, the Club built its first hut on Mt. Madison. The planners chose the high col between Mounts Madison and Adams because it was near Randolph, then New England's hiking center. Most of New England's wildlands, timbered or treeless, belonged to private owners. The Brown Lumber company, which owned thirty thousand acres in the vicinity, donated the one-acre site at Madison. Before settling on Madison, the planners had looked at several sites, but ruled them out. Madison Spring had a prolific water source, was directly accessible from the valley, and was high enough on the Presidential Ridge to afford marvelous day-hiking possibilities.

On or near many White Mountain summits, hotels and corrals had been built. Mounts Washington, Lafayette, Pequaket and Moosilauke, and Pleasant Mountain (in Maine) all bore structures. Some were stone buildings, like Mt. Washington's Tip Top House. Others were wood-framed, like Chocorua's, which blew off the mountain in 1915. Fire claimed many of the rest. Those that remained did a slim business.

Madison was patterned after Europe's famous Alpine huts. But, while those huts could be left without caretakers because many of the local inhabitants were guides who wanted the huts preserved, American huts left without supervision would be ill-treated by local hunters and ignorant or careless hikers. Indeed, as time went by, Madison's wooden floor was torn up for fuel; thereafter, the footing was earth or mud. The wooden wall was finally removed in the search for vermin, leaving the interior damp and chilly.

Although the vandalized hut was far from an ideal refuge, patronage had increased enough by 1906 to justify a small addition, a new room that doubled the hut's capacity. That same year, the Club installed a hutmaster whose presence ensured the proper upkeep of the building and reduced summer vandalism. He sold food supplies, maintained a supply of blankets, and collected fees. As an informal service to overnighters, the hutmaster occasionally prepared meals. When hikers responded enthusiastically to hut cuisine, the meals gradually became more regular. The early concept of hut-as-refuge gave way to a new idea in American recreation: hut-as-hostel.

Encouraged by Madison's success, the AMC undertook construction programs at Carter Notch in 1914, and at Lakes of the Clouds in 1915. So began a period of hut acquisition, construction and renovation. The rapid expansion of the Hut System continued until the early 1930s, but not all attempts worked well. Two years after Lakes of the Clouds was built, the AMC rented a log cabin from the American Realty Company. The cabin (called Imp Hut) was several miles north of Carter Notch in the Carter-Moriah Range. It attracted few hikers, and the Club bailed out after one summer's operation. Later, in 1948, at the urging of the United States Forest Service, Evans Notch Hut was added to the system. The Forest Service provided the building, a brick New England farmhouse known as the Old Brickett Place. Though reachable by road, Evans Notch was eighteen trail miles from Carter Notch. Isolated from the rest of the Hut System, it finally closed in 1957.

Madison, Carter, and Lakes formed the vertices of a triangle.

Midway along its lower leg, the Club built Pinkham Notch Camp shortly after World War I. Pinkham's two cabins centralized the hut operations and would later become the system's year-round headquarters. As the system grew to four huts, it became obvious that some formal oversight was needed. The AMC hired Charles MacIntosh in 1919 as the first paid supervisor of the huts. He was followed soon after by Milton MacGregor, who held the manager's job through 1927. Meanwhile, Pinkham was opened year-round in 1926 under the direction of MacGregor's protégé Joe Dodge.

JOSEPH Brooks Dodge was born in Manchester-by-the-Sea, Massachusetts, on December 28, 1898. Joe was a twentieth-century pioneer, one of the last of those who eked out their existence in a cold and inhospitable backcountry. When he first settled at Pinkham he lived in a log cabin (which he built himself), read by kerosene lamp, and made his toilet outside with water hauled from a nearby river. During the winter he had to ski eleven miles to Gorham for supplies, returning with a hundred-pound load on his back. Joe's speech was as rough as the country he lived in. According to his friend Bill Whitney, "There was no doubt Joe was a churchman. He referred to the Lord in nearly every sentence and in a greater variety of ways than I ever thought to." Yet beneath the gruff exterior was a warmth that won him many friends.

Fishing was one of Joe's passions, and he was not too particular about observing the official season. A young Fish and Game officer, Paul Doherty—now a legendary White Mountain figure—once came close to catching Joe "bending the rules," but Joe was as wily as the trout he was angling for. Seeing the "fish cop" coming, Joe lay down in the tall weeds and Doherty passed by unsuspectingly. A born storyteller, Joe couldn't suppress such a delightful tale. When Doherty asked about it, Joe said, "I ain't goin' to admit a thing, but you better get some glasses."

Joe took his first trip to the White Mountains in 1909: by steamer from Boston to Portland, by train to Glen Station, and by buckboard up through Pinkham Notch over what Joe called "two wheel-ruts in the wilderness." He returned to the Hills after World War I and was appointed Pinkham hutmaster in 1922. In winter he snowshoed to the high huts to mitigate vandalism and to assess the damage done to the huts by storms. Impressed by his zeal and innovation, the Hut Committee named him manager of all the huts in 1928.

Joe Dodge's vision was simple: The White Mountains were a place where thousands of people might have a "healthful and inexpensive vacation on the ridges of New England." He devoted most of his professional life to helping them do so.

One of Joe's pursuits was downhill skiing. Although ski races were held in California in the late 1860s, enthusiasm for the sport waned until the AMC and Joe Dodge helped revive interest in it. Shortly after the Fire Trail was cut in 1930 on the eastern side of Mt. Washington, liftless skiing took a toehold in Tuckerman Ravine. Since then downhill skiing in New Hampshire has become a multi-million dollar business. Many major areas and a score of smaller ones have claimed mountainsides across the North Country. While this has benefited skiers and all those who

equip, feed, house and entertain them, it has done less than benefit those who liked the wildness of the White Mountains. The effort to strike a balance is an ongoing conservation concern.

In 1926 New Hampshire was embroiled in another conservation controversy. It concerned Franconia Notch, a famous national landmark, home of the Old Man of the Mountain, "The Great Stone Face." After the Flume and Profile hotels burned there in 1923, the owners sold 6000 acres of land to timber interests. Fearing the impact of intensive logging, conservationists objected to the sale and began an effort to preserve the forest. Led by the AMC and the Society for the Protection of New Hampshire Forests (a group the AMC had helped create in 1901), the "buy a tree to help save the Notch" campaign raised $200,000 from 15,000 citizens. The State provided matching money, making possible, in 1928, the purchase of the Notch, the Flume Gorge, and other landmarks, including Lonesome Lake.

The Hut System then comprised four huts. Joe Dodge's early concern was not to expand the system but to upgrade the existing huts. With the settlement of the Franconia battle, the AMC told Joe to proceed with plans to build the first hut in the Franconias. A Forest Service representative accompanied Joe and some Club officials to Eagle Lake on Mt. Lafayette, the proposed location. The view won out—north into Canada, west to the Kinsman-Moosilauke range, and south to the foothills, with Franconia Notch 2000 feet immediately below.

The State purchase included several cabins built in 1876. Although the cabins were in ill repair, improvements would make them habitable. Joe saw their potential as links in a chain of huts. The Club leased and began operating the cabins in 1929.

Although the hut builders did not know it then, their hut system would coincide with the Appalachian Trail that Benton MacKaye, a forester and regional planner, dreamed of long before. In 1922, volunteer trail builders constructed the first segments in Palisades Interstate Park, which straddles the New York-New Jersey border. Since many New England footways already existed, it remained only for particular segments to be designated. The existing huts already attracted many hikers, and the completed hut system would claim still more spectacular and fragile spots in prime mountain country. No one knew it in 1930, but the seeds were planted then for a conflict among hut users, backpackers, and backcountry managers—a conflict that would come to a head in the late 1960s.

TO Joe Dodge, what might happen thirty-five years down the line had little bearing on the practical problem at hand—a discontinuous hut chain, with a gap of thirty-odd miles separating Lakes of the Clouds Hut from Greenleaf Hut. He and some AMC officers spent most of fall in 1930 searching the ridge country of the western and northern Pemigewasset territory for two more hut sites. They chose the col between South Twin and Galehead Mountain for one, and a streamside location seven miles east of it in the Zealand Valley for the other. Finished in 1932, Galehead and Zealand completed Joe's plans for the hut chain. Six years after his retirement in 1959, the AMC built one more hut at Mizpah Spring in the southern Presidentials.

Joe's foresight created a system that embraces a pleasing variety of terrain and vistas. Lonesome Lake, the southwestern termi-

nus, is an almost primeval wooded spot in the shadow of Cannon Mountain. From there Greenleaf Hut is four and one-half trail miles. It too overlooks a lake but is near timberline, where the trees are lower, the winds higher, and the ambience more alpine. To reach Galehead you must climb another 1200 feet to the apex of the Franconia Ridge, then descend to Lafayette's north peak. It is an open hike through a world of tiny flowers. The Franconia and Garfield Ridges form a wall around the Pemigewasset territory, a patchwork striped with logging roads, mountain streams and foot trails. A section of the Appalachian Trail continues through a spruce and fir forest, tops bald Mt. Garfield, and ends at Galehead. The hurricane of 1938 downed the last of the big trees—twelve and fifteen inches at the butt—and laid open a mountainscape that makes porch-sitting at Galehead a treat of the first order.

The trail from there to South Twin's summit was cut by a sadist, but once you are there you can see Mt. Washington, still some twenty-odd miles away. The trail stretches out, running through misshapen plateaus where white-throated sparrows chant all day, and right up the broken-rocked side of Guyot into hints of alpine zone. Then down through mile after mile of bunchberry patch, and on to Zeacliff for a wide-open view of the Pemi, where you can look ahead at Mt. Carrigain, geographical center of the White Mountains. A trail through birches twisted by winter snows leads down toward Zealand Valley, and a skinnydip in Zealand Falls for the hardy.

The run from Zealand Hut to Crawford Notch is more than five miles. From Zealand Pond (with outlets at both ends), you follow the old logging railroad grade, occasionally kicking up old ties and spikes, drop down into what Ethan Allen Crawford called "The Notch of the White Mountains," and go up the Crawford Path, opened in 1819. The route continues up over the Southern Peaks into the largest patch of alpine zone in the East. Each of the several summits—Clinton, Franklin, Pleasant (renamed Eisenhower), Monroe—is really an extension of the big one, Mt. Washington, which remains in view all the way up the ridge.

Lakes of the Clouds Hut, hidden on the north side of Monroe, hangs on the edge of the Ammonoosuc Ravine. It is a frail little box ready to blow into the ravine. It almost did one winter when

a 165-mile-an-hour wind sucked off a forty-foot section of the roof and scattered it across the headwall.

The route to Madison is seven miles, all above timberline, across rocky trails laid down at the turn of the century by one of America's best-trail builders, J. Rayner Edmands. The ridge is wide open to the prevailing wind, which dumps hail, rain, even snow in the summer. On a good day Madison is six hours or so away for the average hiker. The hut lies in a little col, has its own frigid lake, a colony of cotton grass, mountain sandwort, some black crowberry, and alpine goldenrod.

When you leave the col, you descend into the Great Gulf by any of several trails that range from steep and scary to only mildly dangerous. The Osgood Trail brings you into Carter Notch Hut and Pinkham Notch Camp. Carter is crammed into a narrow, rocky notch that holds a rock glacier, ice caves, and a gothic boulder field called the "Ramparts." Once you could walk another score miles to Evans Notch Hut, but with that gone, Carter is the end of the system. Cozy, quiet Carter, the hutmen call it. A fine place to stop after an eight-day traverse.

WHEN he left the AMC in 1959, Joe Dodge had much to look back on, but his greatest contribution was the introduction of travel-light hiking to the White Mountains. Hikers in Yosemite's High Sierra had begun the practice in 1916 by relying on fixed camps for food and bedding. The now popular art of backpacking got off to an early start some twenty years later—again in the western wilderness. Its advocates prefer to camp out with equipment from the growing array of ever-lighter gear. Hut advocates like to go lighter still, mixing amenities with wildness and sharing experiences with companions equally in love with the mountains. Joe was their great benefactor.

In 1955, Dartmouth College recognized Joe Dodge's singular contribution to recreation in the state of New Hampshire by presenting him an honorary degree. President John S. Dickey said:

"One-time wireless operator at sea, long-time mountaineer, student of Mt. Washington weather, you have been more than a match for storms, slides, fools, skiers and porcupines. You have rescued so many of us from both the harshness of the mountain and the soft ways leading down to boredom that you, yourself,

are now beyond rescue as a legend of all that is unafraid, friendly, rigorously good and ruggedly expressive in the out-of-doors. . . . As one New Hampshire institution to another, Dartmouth delights to acknowledge you as Master of Arts."

When Joe Dodge retired to his home in the broad Intervale he loved to call "The Valley of the Saco," he became more active in community affairs. Perhaps his favorite activity was the morning weather show he hosted on a local radio station. Joe had always been interested in weather—so interested that in 1932 he had co-founded the Mt. Washington Observatory, which continues to supply information to meteorologists. But Joe wasn't choosy about his weather; whenever someone asked him if the day's weather might be *bad*, Joe would respond, "All weather is *good* weather, some's just different." For the benefit of his radio listeners, though, Joe devised a rating system. The bottom end of the scale was the rainy day, which Joe called a "five-center" (Saco Valley citizens were supposed to deposit the day's value in their Joe Dodge piggy banks). A great day, when you could pick out the spruces atop the Moat Range, was a "fifty-center."

Joe died of a heart attack in October 1973, having just settled into his living room chair after a fishing trip with two friends. When word of his death spread, tributes poured in from the periodicals that had all but canonized him during his lifetime. Probably the most eloquent statement, as brief and direct as Joe might have made it, was broadcast from Mt. Washington: His friend Willy Harris said, "Joe had about as many friends as there are trees in New Hampshire."

Hundreds of Joe's friends packed into the church to participate in the memorial services. Later, his ashes would join his wife Teen's high up in the Moat Range where you could look up to see Mt. Washington and down to see the Valley of the Saco. Joe would have called the day of the service a fifty-center.

THE hut system has changed little since Joe's times. And the mountains endure, thanks mostly to nature's vigor, but also to the energies of the Forest Service, the Appalachian Mountain Club, and other conservation groups. The hut system is an important component of the husbanding effort because it concentrates the impact of thousands of users, an especially significant function in sensitive alpine areas. Still, it is not easy to settle the arguments among those who claim that huts degrade the environment more than camping does and those who believe huts are easier on the land.

In any event, huts do more than provide bunks and meals for hikers. They are also educational centers, at which the AMC sponsors a series of workshops each year. Many are oriented toward teachers, who learn to use the mountain environment as a classroom. Others are conducted in and around the huts in mountain ecology, mycology, geology, photography, natural history, mountain medicine, and astronomy. Several mountain leadership courses are offered, and many huts have resident naturalists who lead natural history hikes.

If the huts have any most important educational function, it's that they teach us to accept and learn from the austerity of wildlands. Aldo Leopold saw the American outdoorsman "draped with an infinity of contraptions, all offered as aids to our self-reliance, hardihood, woodcraft, or marksmanship, but too often functioning as substitutes for them." The exponential growth in gadgetry has continued since Leopold's death, and few have shared his perception of what our artifacts, carried into the backcountry, do to it and to us. We are only now discovering that the amenities that have made wilderness accessible are making its meaning increasingly inaccessible. Henry Thoreau understood the meaning of wildness and recognized it as the preservation of the world. He said that man has only four "necessaries": food, clothing, shelter and fuel—fuel for the heart and head that is. The huts provide those essentials, and little more.

For nearly a century the AMC Hut System has helped people enjoy White Mountain wildness, in fragments if not in wholeness. Hundreds of thousands have learned to be at home in the wild. They have also learned that absolute wilderness has shrunk absolutely, and that the chances for preserving what remains of it increase markedly as more people experience what John Burroughs called "the wilderness state of mind." If the huts can give hikers an inkling of what the wholeness must have been like, they will have served their function.

There is a clear tendency in American conservation to relegate to government all necessary jobs that private landowners fail to perform. . . . Most of this growth in governmental conservation is proper and logical, some of it is inevitable. That I imply no disapproval is implicit in the fact that I have spent most of my life working for it. Nevertheless the question arises: what is the ultimate magnitude of the enterprise? . . . At what point will governmental conservation, like the mastodon, become handicapped by its own dimensions?

—ALDO LEOPOLD

Lightning

PAIN wound around Greg Sherblom's body like roots around a rock. The chaos of the electrical storm abated somewhat as he left his weakened friend in the pup tent and stumbled blindly from the rock foundation that sheltered them. Sherblom stood for a moment, chest heaving, and tried to regain his bearings. "I'm on Mount Lafayette," he thought, "5000 feet above sea level, miles from any help." For a moment he panicked. The thought recurred: *miles from help*. Then he remembered: Greenleaf Hut; they can call a helicopter and save my friend.

He hesitated again, rubbing his shoulder, looking desperately for a trail. Lafayette's treeless summit offered little clue. Many locations on the mountain looked identical in clear weather. And now, in the mist of a settling storm, visibility was cut to a few yards. Granite, loose rock and dirt gave him no point of reference, but Sherblom found a trail sign: Greenleaf Trail to Greenleaf Hut, 1.2 miles. Precious seconds had been lost in indecision, but now that he had a direction, he began the descent.

The rocks, dangerous in the rain, stood as fuzzy gray obstacles scarcely visible in the waning light. During the half-hour descent he stumbled and fell several times, but righted himself and lunged ahead from rock to unstable rock. One leg became numb, and each step sent bolts of pain through his good leg. Then, in the easing rain, the tired boy looked up to see Greenleaf Hut on the opposite shore of a small alpine lake. His cry for help roused some lakeside campers, who helped him across the last stretch.

The hut door opened and Lennie Bannos, a camper, helped Sherblom inside. He stood drenched and shivering as he described the plight of his friend Stewart Putnam. A spasm of pain contorted his face and body, and he was led away to recover from his own ordeal.

Earlier the day had borne omens of a storm. Sticky heat crept up and enveloped the Franconia Ridge, but the thunderheads were slow to form. From Greenleaf that morning I had seen uncountable ridges toward Vermont and Canada. The closer ones were a deep green, those in the middle distance a faded blue, which in turn gave way to the gray of the farthest ridges. At the horizon, mountain and sky were indistinguishable.

But other mountains were more immediate. Behind me, a thousand feet above Greenleaf, rose Lafayette's main summit. Loose granite and red dirt, the mass of this major summit of the Franconia Range supports a spine-like ridge that runs for miles to the south and vanishes in the wilderness that sheds the Pemigewasset River. The Old Bridle Path, formerly a horsepath, now a foot trail, ascends to the spine on a soaring buttress known as the Agony Ridge. At spots along the Bridle Path, the ridge drops off steeply into the Walker Ravine. Though precipitous, the trail had never been a problem for us. Each crewman had so often descended and climbed the Agony Ridge that the trail had become a part of him. We knew its turns, rises, depressions, washouts. Every step and handhold was etched in our minds.

Dana Whiting and Tom Loucks had packed the Bridle Path at least as often as I had, and my assistant, Mike Bridgewater, with a previous year's experience at Greenleaf, knew the trail better than the rest of us. Lew McKeon was new man in the hut and, though unfamiliar with hut routine and packing, he picked up the craft quickly. We were a close bunch, and we got closer as the summer went on. We were young—not a man over twenty-one—and very much in love with the mountains. It was a sharing summer; the good and not-so-good times belonged to each of us. And the good times, of course, prevailed.

THAT day, July 22, 1967, found Mike, Dana and Tom in the valley and Lew a substitute packer at Galehead Hut, eight miles away. As hutmaster at Greenleaf, I was responsible for setting up the work schedule and assigning the crew its various tasks. The cooking chores were mine that day, so I remained in the hut alone while those whose turn it was to pack supplies rumbled off into Franconia Notch that morning. It would be a tough day to hike, I thought: warm in the morning, a thunder storm likely in the afternoon.

In the lethargy that often comes with sticky heat, my thoughts ran to the crew. They would be edging upward, each carrying about one hundred pounds, cursing the load, the trail and the heat. I imagined them perspiring profusely, arcs of dampness circling under the arms of their shirts, shorts becoming wet and clinging. Then, if the day were similar to those of most other storms, the weather would doublecross them. After they had found the rhythm of packing, become accustomed to the load, the heat and the climb, the afternoon sky would darken and enshroud them in cold air until the rain came.

But it held off. The weather was seductive. It seemed to dare anyone to walk the flanks of the hill without getting wet. Surely the rain would come, and lightning; it should have been obvious to anyone. The crew members were aware of it as they arrived at the hut with their loads, and many hikers also sensed it and came to Greenleaf to seek shelter from the impending storm. But others had decided that the storm would not arrive until they had safely completed their hikes. These lit out to climb the ridge and run along its back before descending quickly on the Falling Waters Trail. Among those who took the dare were two seventeen-year-old boys who had passed through Greenleaf earlier in the day.

When the rain finally came, it was not an idyllic summer shower that swept the lush scent of the green land up from the valley. The clouds boiled and heaved, pulling a massive black cloak over the range. Then rain came lancelike from the sky.

Unknown to us, a potential tragedy was unfolding on the ridge. Gregory Sherblom and Stewart Putnam had decided earlier that afternoon not to cross the ridge and hike down to Franconia. Instead, on arriving at Lafayette's summit, the pair had chosen to camp at the foundation of the old summit house. Both inexperienced mountaineers, they set themselves unknowingly on a 5000-foot lightning rod.

Near 5:30 p.m., when the temperatures dropped and the thunderheads appeared, Sherblom and Putnam crawled into their small canvas and prepared to weather the storm. The July rain assailed the vast expanse of the Pemigewasset Wilderness to the east and the tiny warm hut a thousand feet below and west of the peak. But the tent, in a lull like the eye of a hurricane, was rained on only slightly. Thunder slammed and roared about them and, as it drew closer, was amplified by the sounding board slopes of the Franconias. Putnam was restless and turned from his prostrate position to his side.

Then lightning!

Sherblom and Putnam felt a searing pain that triggered intense muscle spasms, but somehow neither died instantly from the jolt. Putnam sprang from the warm sleeping bag and began to run uncontrollably in circles. By some uncanny presence of mind, Sherblom, who had also bolted from the tent, regained his faculties despite the pain, and wrapped his friend in his sleeping bag again. Putnam turned blue and vomited. As the rain eased Sherblom, in shock, ran wildly toward Greenleaf Hut.

Ironically, the boy reached the hut during one of those odd moments of complete peace that follow the fiercest parts of storms. With a resilience like that of trampled moss, the smell of the mountain flora sprang up as soon as the rain had slackened. Though chilly, the air had a warm character to it, one of sounds and sights as well as smells: white-throated sparrows sang and black ravens circled above in silence.

From the confusion created by Greg Sherblom's entrance, a picture of the situation gradually emerged. Someone, a guest at Greenleaf, entered the kitchen and announced that the boy had just run down from Lafayette's peak with the news that his buddy was severely hurt by lightning. Sherblom was writhing on a mattress when I entered the bunkroom. Even in his pain and shock, however, he thought only of Putnam, who might be dead by now. An eery tingle ran up my back as this ghostly young man pleaded with me to get a helicopter. I told him we would do what we could, though inside I felt that his companion was probably dead.

In the goofer room, the main dining and gathering place in each hut, things were still agitated. It was meal hour, but there was no time for food. I called for volunteers to help us with the stokes litter. (Helicopters were simply not available then, and even now the bulk of AMC rescue work is done by hut crews and volunteers.) Several men offered their help. Flashlights would be necessary, and waterproof clothing and parkas. Meanwhile the crew made ready with first aid gear, ropes and blankets, while I called Pinkham Notch Camp on the radio.

During the hasty preparations one of the crew exclaimed that we had no litter! He was right; the litter was down in the valley at the Cannon Mountain Tramway, where we had left it after transporting a victim down the Skookumchuck Trail two days earlier. It was my blunder. I had judged that we were too fatigued to carry it back to the hut after that rescue. Now we regretted my decision. As nothing in the hut even resembled a litter, we decided to take AMC packboards, hoping that at some time the notified AMC and US Forest Service people would arrive with the litter we had requested by radio.

In the valley, the radio call had immediate consequences. Dr. Harry McDade, dining at the house of some friends in nearby Littleton, New Hampshire, excused himself from the meal when he was advised of the accident by Pinkham Notch. Franconia Notch State Park and Forest Service personnel were alerted, and they began the three-mile trek to Greenleaf, as did several AMC employees dispatched from Pinkham.

Mike and Dana set out for the summit with the pack boards and first aid gear. Before making the portable two-way radio ready for travel, I ran into the women's bunkroom for something.

There, with his hands in his pockets and head down, stood a middle-aged man who had chosen to hide rather than admit squarely that he would not help with the litter. Perhaps he had excellent reason for hiding; he may have been ill or exhausted. He mumbled something in excuse. I replied, "Okay," and left.

Activity in the goofer room had not subsided. Male volunteers quickly packed their rain gear and flashlights. A female doctor who had descended from Lafayette earlier that day, and who was too exhausted to make another trip to the summit, agreed to attend to Sherblom. A friend of mine from home, Kathy Stein, and another kind woman offered to salvage supper and keep something warm for the rescuers. Then, with most ends tied up, I ran outside, made a test call on the radio, and began to climb. The sky that had so recently been menacing was, for the moment at least, peaceful.

THE first hundred yards of the trip to the summit is a quick descent to the shore of Eagle Lake and an equally abrupt climb through a small canyon of soft scrub. Several guests picking their way up through the scrub let me pass. I was moving at a pace which, for me, was fast: face down, eyes on the boulders, a steady mechanical march up the mountain. Tommy and Dana, who were carrying most of the rescue gear, were just ahead. With a lighter load I soon overtook them, and they stepped aside to let me puff by.

My body began to protest: no wind; sore, slow muscles; wondering when I'd feel human again. *Quit.* I stopped for a moment and then began again. Some long minutes later, where the trail breaks above the real treeline, I stopped again, feeling guilty about my weakness. It is at times like this that you coldly realize your personal frailties are consequential. The thought of resting longer tugs seductively at you. It is a selfish thought and must be resisted, you tell yourself. *Push yourself, a boy's life is in the balance.* Afraid that the boy might already be dead, I half hiked, half ran past Phil Morgan, a former Greenleaf man, who had stopped for a rest. Up through the mud and over the red talus, which lay on the upper reaches of the mountain like shards of a broken earthenware vase.

The prospect of another death was chilling. As I approached the summit, images of the previous year's death on Mount Webster returned: the litter, a radio call, a frightened old man bearing the news, the trail fire flickering a morbid glow on the body. But most of all the taste of death, there in my mouth, resurrected. Again I was blowing air through the old man's lips, feeling the stubble of his man's face against my chin, smelling the dead, stale air exhaled back at me. I remembered that I had been horrified by the idea that the gasses and juices of the corpse might be inside me, and so had spat continuously that night in a feeble effort to retch out the whole idea of the death, to cleanse myself.

Although only twenty minutes had passed between leaving the hut and arriving at the false peak just yards below the summit, it seemed much longer, the trip measured not in time but in breath and energy and anticipation of what lay up in the rocks ahead. As the summit foundation came into sight, I tried to

shout, but failed. Breathless, I stopped and called weakly. No answer. I hiked again, faster than before, calling, stumbling, listening. Finally a reply came from the granite blocks. *He is alive!* Clambering over the last rocks of the summit, I reached a grassy ledge, on which, some yards way, sat a little pup tent. Beside it kneeled a dark-haired boy. He was not Putnam.

"He's all right," said the unidentified hiker crouched over the flattened figure. The boy attending Putnam had started for the summit when he had learned of the situation. It was fortunate that he had reached the victim quickly, but disconcerting that he had not waited for the rest of the party. Had the rescue team been forced to turn back, he too might have been stranded on the summit. In his eagerness to help, he had risked compounding the emergency.

Putnam moaned. Twisting, arching in his sleeping bag, he turned his face to me. A light blue pallor emphasized its slim outline, and his hair looked incongruously in order. The eyes were tight, unopened, like deep lines cut in a ball of gray putty. I asked him to open them. His pupils were of equal size: no concussion evident. He breathed easily.

"Where do you hurt?" I asked.

"All over . . . What time is it?"

"Almost seven o'clock."

"Morning or night?" he asked.

"Night." Perhaps there was a concussion, I thought.

Phil Morgan walked through the rock passage that formed the entryway to the foundation, and after him, not minutes later, steamed Dana, Tommy and Mike. The others filtered in gradually until our forces numbered ten—hardly an adequate rescue team.

A pall of yellow mist floated just over the summit. It was warm as we grouped at the foundation. I tried to raise Mizpah Hut on the radio, but Lakes of the Clouds came in, Duncan Wannamaker's voice. I asked if he knew the whereabouts of the Forest Service and the litter we had requested. Pinkham had instructed him to assure us that the litter and extra forces were on their way. I realized that no intervention, human or divine, would speed their ascent.

But the fate that had granted a lull now began to conspire against us. The weather turned foul again; darkness was fast approaching; and still no sign of the Forest Service litter. The summit had to be evacuated, and quickly.

Mike and Phil began building a litter of two pack boards, a couple of hardwood tent poles left by some obliging campers, and pack rope. Meanwhile, Tommy and Dana worked on another litter, this one a net fashioned from the gold-line climbing rope Tommy had remembered to bring. The others readied themselves for the descent and helped us put Putnam into an envelope of two sleeping bags, extra blankets, and the final shell, the pup tent.

The litters had to be tested before we could decide which to use. Although the pack board litter was the stiffer, it would almost certainly break where the two packs joined. The net by itself would be difficult to control, Putnam would be dragged intermittently, and there would be few locations on the trail where we could set the litter when the rescuers needed rest. We decided to combine the two litters, the pack boards forming a platform for the victim, Loucky's net a hammock for the boards.

Now we were ready: four crewmen, one old hutman, five volunteers and an injured boy, in a struggle with a mountain and a storm determined to make its mark on everyone. Clouds churned overhead, obscuring what had been visible of the Pemi, the Walker Ravine and the Franconia Ridge. I called Lakes once more to tell Dunc we were getting the hell out of there.

FROM the foundation entrance stretches a rubble of coconut-sized rocks, a slanted stage fifty yards wide. At its edge, ten litter bearers turned to look back at the summit, now obscured by a veil of rain. As if on cue, one more blast of lightning struck the highest point of the rock, burning on our retinas a negative image that lasted for several seconds. The image faded, but not the thought that the last bolt could have killed Stewart Putnam.

We dropped below the tilted plateau and muscled the litter through a narrow passage of boulders. The entire scape above tree line was a redundancy of rock slides, loose gravel and prohibitive gullies. Transporting a litter over this is a grueling chore for a litter party of twenty-five strong men. And if the weather is foul, the difficulties are multiplied. The litter itself is trail width, and the six to eight men who carry it must climb over, around and through all obstacles along the trail. In a normal party, the group splits into units, each one carrying the cargo for a spell, then shifting off for a rest. But we had a dearth of porters and a Rube Goldberg litter!

Mountain weather is capricious, and that is both its most brutal characteristic and the essence of its beauty. One moment the sky is clear, the air warm; the next minute, the sun is driven away by rain, hail, even snow. That day the mountain weather conspired with fatigue, hunger and darkness to compound the toll on the bearers. The Greenleaf Trail was nearly invisible, so we fell easily on the water-slimed rocks. But we pushed forward and down through the gnawing wind, sustained only by the grim urgency of the mission and the prospect of food and shelter.

These comforts, though, were still far off. For now, the only respite came between steps, at rest stops, when we could momentarily forget about Putnam's pain and the miserable chill in the air. An old man was our headlights. Taciturn and humble, he did what he could without complaint. Nine others inched after him, leaning out from the bowed litter. We found a union in the struggle—ten men working closely together, performing the same function, with the same recognition of purpose. Never before had the crew experienced the feeling of total necessity, of being the only people capable of performing a vital service.

I slipped on a rock, snapping the reverie I'd fallen into. Our rhythm was upset, and eight men absorbed a fraction more of the boy's weight. I recovered, and we stopped once again to rest and assess our progress; it was uncompromisingly slow. Nearly an hour and a half had passed since our leaving the summit, and still no sign of extra people. Below us was the greater mass of Lafayette, and through the shifting clouds the faint gas lights of Greenleaf Hut flickered tauntingly.

The litter sagged. Its ropes were loose, and the platform bent into a long V. Putnam was less comfortable than when we had begun the descent, but he managed some half naps during the smooth going. Remembering Doc McDade's admonition that a sleeping victim might never waken, I frequently forced the boy to talk. Unsure of the severity of his condition, we tried to keep him warm and reasonably clear-headed.

The chances of his dying from exposure were not remote. Many climbers had died from exposure, even in temperatures

TRAVELLERS IN A STORM, MOUNT WASHINGTON.

well above freezing. So I was not amused when Mike Bridge-water thought it appropriate to supply comic relief. With each bolt of lightning he cried, "We're going to get fried!" After the fourth time, I snapped, "Shut up!" Perhaps that abrupt censure did not represent everyone's feelings, but I was certain that Stewart Putnam wanted to hear something else, anything else.

At tree line, the party met special problems. The trail, though less steep than on the bare slopes above, was narrower and wetter. Leaning trees impeded progress and showered us with droplets collected during the storm. But we were nearing the knoll a few hundred yards from the hut.

Finally we heard a voice—a voice from *up* the hill! Lew Mc-

Keon, Greenleaf's fifth man identified himself. He had started from Galehead Hut and had sought cover somewhere between Garfield Pond and Lafayette when the electrical storm broke. We desperately needed his help, so he shed his pack board and grabbed a corner of the load.

Arriving at the crest of the knoll, we were surprised to see only a weak light in the hut windows. The gas lights had gone out, and someone had thoughtfully replaced them with candles. Mike ran down to change the gas cylinders and make ready for the litter party. On his way he passed Howey Parker, a college chum of mine and the first of the US Forest Service to arrive, and Dr. Harry McDade.

Harry gave Putnam a cursory examination and then took a corner of the litter himself. Ten wet, crawling, stumbling minutes later, Putnam had been pronounced okay and put to bed in our crew room.

Greenleaf was a mess. Counting rescue help from Pinkham, Franconia Notch State Park, and the Forest Service, the tiny hut held fifty people, most of them chilled and famished. The hut was cluttered with hikers, gear, dishes, and mud tracked in by the rescuers. Most of the Forest Service people were sipping hot chocolate by candlelight when we ushered young Putnam in through the kitchen door. They were resting in preparation for carrying the victims to Franconia that night. But the preliminary diagnosis indicated that the boys would probably be able to hike down to the valley the next day, with Forest Service help if necessary.

So we ate. Slowly and quietly, neither able nor willing to put the day's events in perspective. Afterwards we went to bed, squeezing into whatever padded spaces we could find.

MORNING came too quickly, and with it the chore of preparing breakfast for the biggest house of the summer. We managed the task, but not with the usual pride and fire of Greenleaf tradition. After breakfast the exodus began: Putnam and Sherblom, escorted by Harry and the Forest Service, then State Park people, Pinkham people, and finally our guests. We thanked everyone as they filed out.

The crew was alone. Time for our meal, crew chow. There was a conspicuous silence at the table as we thought over the most profound night of our lives. Two boys had almost died. One was scarred by lightning that had struck the ground forty feet from where he lay. The current had travelled through wires of water and burned him at every point of contact with the ground, leaving permanent spider-like welts where the electricity had coagulated the blood in capillaries near his skin. Yet fortune had spared him. Had he been lying on his back or stomach rather than on his side, the current might have gone through his heart and killed him. Thanks to his friend Sherblom's grit, we had been able to take advantage of a lull in the storm and bring the victim to safety. And we'd been helped by many unnamed people who had sacrificed in order to save a human life.

I looked around at Mike, Dana, Tommy and Lew. There was no need to articulate what we felt. The inexplicable fraternal sense that is really the essence of a summer in the mountains was keen inside us. We had never been closer to each other. Or, paradoxically, to our mountain. On its flanks we felt the ecstasy of insignificance. We knew what it was to live in the province of something bigger, that near-religious feeling that comes with absorbing in a small way some of the monumental strength and stability of the mountains.

These feelings are shared by mountaingoers of all generations. Later that summer I shared a bottle of wine with Carl Blanchard on some rocks in front of the hut. Day was fading, light thinning, and we were looking up at the serrated ridge, the knuckled fist of our mountain. Carl had been hutmaster at Greenleaf in the 1930s, so we reminisced, as hutmen do. A chill began to ripple in both of us, only partly from the cold and the wine. Carl was silently recounting his summers, and so was I; it was that tacit understanding that really caused the chills. The events of our summers passed as lambent clouds over the surfaces of our minds. One especially rose large and mute in my mind. We knew without speaking what a hutman's summer is. Despite the years between us, we shared alike in the feast of gray shadows before us.

We toasted and watched darkness come.

Drawn by I. Sprague.   Lith. Boston.

MOUNT WASHINGTON, FROM THE SUMMIT OF MT PLEASANT.

The joy of being in the mountains is that every unused or waiting faculty of our higher nature is strained to the utmost to interpret them in the language of the spirit. . . . Great as the gift as to some, the use of the mountains to lift us into higher moods of life is common to us all. Like the air and the sky and the clouds and the sunlight, no one can lay exclusive claims to them. The unlikeness begins in the fitness of the spirit to interpret them.

—Julius Ward

The mountains should not be our enemy. How distasteful it is to read of a man "throwing down the gauntlet" to them, setting out to "conquer," speaking of them as enemies against whom he pits his own strength! Mountaineering is not a battle, nor a state of war, for such things are mere fleeting episodes. Its foundation is always a pure love of nature and of mountains, the sinking of self in their life, their being, their spirit. Even if such phrases are merely meant to be picturesque, there is a note of arrogance and presumption, like the boastful chatter of dwarfs. Modesty is the greatest virtue of the mountaineer. The mountains are so great, so forbearing, so patient. Many a victory, which seems to shed its light upon man's energy and skill, is yet due to their benevolence. They were quietly watching, in no wise hindering, their tremendous armour laid aside. But once they rouse themselves to fight in earnest, their aim is sure and devastating. What man of understanding will picture himself stronger than they? I cannot imagine any place less suitable to choose than the high mountains, wherein to display the mastery of mankind.

—JULIUS KUGY

The time has been that these wild solitudes,
Yet beautiful as wild, were trod by me
Oftener than now; and when the ills of life
Had chafed my spirit—when the unsteady pulse
Beat with strange flutterings—I would wander forth
And seek the woods. The sunshine on my path
Was to me as a friend. The swelling hills,
The quiet dells retiring far between,
With gentle invitation to explore
Their windings, were a calm society
That talked with me and soothed me. Then the chant
of birds, and chime of brooks, and soft caress
Of the fresh sylvan air, made me forget
The thoughts that broke my peace, and I began
To gather simples by the fountain's brink,
And lose myself in daydreams. While I stood
In nature's loneliness, I was with one
With whom I early grew familiar, one
Who never had a frown for me, whose voice
Never rebuked me for the hours I stole
From cares I loved not, but of which the world
Deems highest, to converse with her.

—WILLIAM CULLEN BRYANT
A Winter Piece

THE SOUND OF THE TREES

I wonder about the trees.
Why do we wish to bear
Forever the noise of these
More than another noise
So close to our dwelling place?
We suffer them by the day
Till we lose all measure of pace,
And fixity in our joys,
And acquire a listening air.
They are that that talks of going
But never gets away;
And that talks no less for knowing,
As it grows wiser and older,
That now it means to stay.
My feet tug at the floor
And my head sways to my shoulder
Sometimes when I watch trees sway,
From the window or the door.
I shall set forth for somewhere,
I shall make the reckless choice
Some day when they are in voice
And tossing so as to scare
The white clouds over them on.
I shall have less to say,
But I shall be gone.

—ROBERT FROST

. . .You must come to this place more than once if you expect to have your mind filled with any thing more than the perception of a brilliant cloud; come, if you want to feel the beauty and the variety of the scenery. Come, as a resident, calm, observing, sedate. . . . No country is well known till after a second visit. We return with minds furnished with new powers for observation. Fresh objects start up, and new beauties disclose themselves. We go away, it seems, only to sharpen our faculties, and obtain a fresh relish for new objects of delight. . . .

—NATHAN HALE

And then I steadily ascended along a rocky ridge half clad with stinted trees, where wild beasts haunted, till I lost myself quite in the upper air clouds, seeming to pass an imaginary line which separates a hill, mere earth heaped up, from a mountain, into a super-terranean grandeur and sublimity. . . . It can never become familiar; you are lost the moment you set foot there.

—HENRY DAVID THOREAU

Our mountains are large enough for all the experiences possible to men on mountains and for all the associations men have ever had with them. The Sandwich mountains have taken their toll of human life by forest fires and by hard weather. They have resounded to the roar of logs shot down in chutes, and to those going out of rivers in spring freshets. They furnish big game shooting, even a moose now and then. They have trails and shelters and a storied past. Romance haunts them as surely as it does the Trossachs or the Schwarzwald or the Pyrenees. It is a romance of an Indian past and of white pioneers; it is a romance of a heyday when American life was at the top of being; it is a romance of a present of abandoned farms, or half-tilled farms, from which a stock of racy and poetic speech is quickly passing. It was a rich civilization that flourished here, and that is even now not wholly gone. That civilization is preserved to us not by tradition only or by survivals only. Old letters and old diaries that have come my way bear testimony to it on every page. Chocorua, the Indian chief, has his place in the romance, and Hannah Dustin, the slayer of Indians, and thousands of men and women, unhonored now and unsung, who knew wonder and delight in town and village, hill farm or interval manor, and adventure and love, and sorrow and the menace of the years. All that life has to give has been lived where now are only cellar holes and lilac bushes to tell of homes and school-houses, town halls and churches. The romance of the past has not all of it been forgotten either, for old folks in back-country places have long memories. They tell the traditional stories of the countryside over and over, so often indeed, that nearly all our remembered by some one or other of the many who have listened to them. . . . It is Robert Frost who is the chief revealer of our farm folks and villagers, in those woodwind tones of his that are so exactly those of the English horn. It is he who has expressed that menace to which I have referred as so often present at autumn days' ends and overclouded hours, "the menace of winter and evening coming on together."

By what citations or specimens or cross-sections can I quickly put before you the look and life of New Hampshire; characteristic hours and landscape, the quality of air and tumbling water, the houses and ways of people? . . . I must get down quickly a few more distinguishing characteristics and have done. It is a country of short summers. There are no more than three weeks between hyla calls and cricket song. It is a country where new and old meet in quietness and peace. When your car gets stuck in the mud, oxen drag it out. It is a country of contrasts and surprises. Call on one of your neighbors and you find the whole family in the barn thrashing beans, two bearskins of deepest black curing on the great timbers that support the roof, great Herefords at ease in the tie-ups, and a spanking south wind driving wafts of the scent of clover bloom in at the barn door. Call on another neighbor and note from the northern window Whiteface brooding above its abandoned farms, with mists rising here, and each ridge and bowl sharply revealed over there in the hard light.

Even more briefly I must crowd in other of the moments and moods and attributes of the White Mountains if I am to give you a half notion of them. I must get into these pages sunlight, and the sound of wind, and ruddy life. I must get in bleakness and northernness and wintriness. I must get in the wild, the sinister, the menacing. I must get in the restful, the comforting, the healing. I must get into the writing the loon's cry, the barking of the great horned owl, the demoniac scream of the wildcat; the twittering of swallows in the barn at noon, the far crying of crows in the gray of the morning, the lowing of cattle coming home on the edge of evening. I must have in this book dark forests of spruce, and lake water, and granite-ledged mountains. I must have in it plowed fields and hominess and lamplight in windows at the fall of night. Such intimations of White Mountain summers as these recorded have come to me recurrently at various hours of the thousand and five hundred days I have spent in New Hampshire. I was happy in my dream of the mountains, forested in red and gold, with high shoulders and ridges and peaks white with snow, and far away, and beyond the night. I am happy now in what I know of them from unhurried days among them. The White Mountains seemed to me, in childhood, as I listened to my folks' tales of them, our American land of romance. They are largely that to me still, after years of intimacy, and as instant to the heart in their reality as a dream-come-true.

—CORNELIUS WEYGANDT
The White Hills

References

Appalachia, published by the Appalachian Mountain Club since 1876, and Appalachia Bulletin, carry articles on the White Mountains, their natural and social histories, management, environmental education, wilderness philosophy, legislative action, and adventure. Appalachia is indexed.

Other AMC publications include: The AMC White Mountain Guide (1976); AMC Field Guide to Mountain Flowers of New England (1977 edition), by Stuart Harris, Frederick Steele, Miriam Underhill, and Jean Langenheim; and AMC Field Guide to Trail Building and Maintenance (1977), by Robert D. Proudman.

The extensive literature on the White Mountains includes: Allen H. Bent's Bibliography of the White Mountains (1911, c1971); The White Hills: Their Legends, Landscapes, and Poetry (1859-1860), by Thomas Starr King; Lucy Crawford's History of the White Mountains (1846, c1966), edited by Stearns Morse; Chronicles of the White Mountains (1916), by Frederick W. Kilbourne; The Book of the White Mountains (1930), by John Anderson and Stearns Morse; The White Hills in Poetry (1912), edited by Eugene R. Musgrove; Bradford on Mount Washington (1928), by Bradford Washburn; William O. Douglas's My Wilderness: East to Katahdin (1961); "The Friendly Huts of the White Mountains," by Justice Douglas, in National Geographic, August 1961; Edward Hoagland's Walking the Dead Diamond River (1973); Paul Bruns's A New Hampshire Everlasting and Unfallen (1969), and Whose Woods These Are: The Story of the National Forests (1962), by Michael Frome. Good texts on natural history are: The Appalachians (1965), by Maurice Brooks; A Guide to New England's Landscape (1971), by Neil Jorgensen; Alpine Zone of the Presidential Range (1964), by L. C. Bliss; The Geology of the Mount Washington Quadrangle (1963), by Marland P. Billings et al; Franconia Notch: An In-Depth Guide (1975), edited by Diane Kostecke; Mount Washington, A Guide and Short History (1973), by Peter Randall; and New Hampshire's Land, a special issue of New Hampshire Profiles, edited by Peter Randall Germane. U.S. Forest Service publications are: Forest Plan, White Mountain National Forest (1974); Guide for Managing National Forests in New England (1970); Search for Solitude (1970); and High Mountain Huts, A Planning Guide (n.d.), by William Reifsnyder.

Relevant Conservation Foundation books are: National Parks for the Future (1972) and The Lands Nobody Wanted (1977), by William Shand and Robert Healy.

In addition to the titles published in its series, The Earth's Wild Places (see verso of front endpaper), Friends of the Earth (U.S.), its associate, Earth Island Ltd., and its sister organizations in many other countries have published books on environmental subjects, including several on the subject of energy, the enterprising search for which constitutes a major environmental threat. Most are written by or contributed to by Amory Lovins: Eryri, the Mountains of Longing; Only One Earth: The Stockholm Conference; Openpit Mining; World Energy Strategies; Non-nuclear Futures; Soft Energy Paths: Toward a Durable Peace; Progress As If Survival Mattered; Sun! A Handbook for the Solar Decade; Soft Path Questions and Answers (in press).

FOE also publishes Not Man Apart semimonthly and ECO occasionally, at conferences of international environmental importance.

Addresses: AMC, 5 Joy Street, Boston, Massachusetts 02108
FOE, 124 Spear St., San Francisco, California 94105

The book is set in Centaur and Arrighi by Mackenzie-Harris Corporation, San Francisco. Separations, lithography, and binding by Arnoldo Mondadori Editore, Verona, Italy, on coated paper made by Cartiera Celdit and Bamberger Kaliko Fabrik. The layout is by Stephen Lyons. The design is by David Brower.

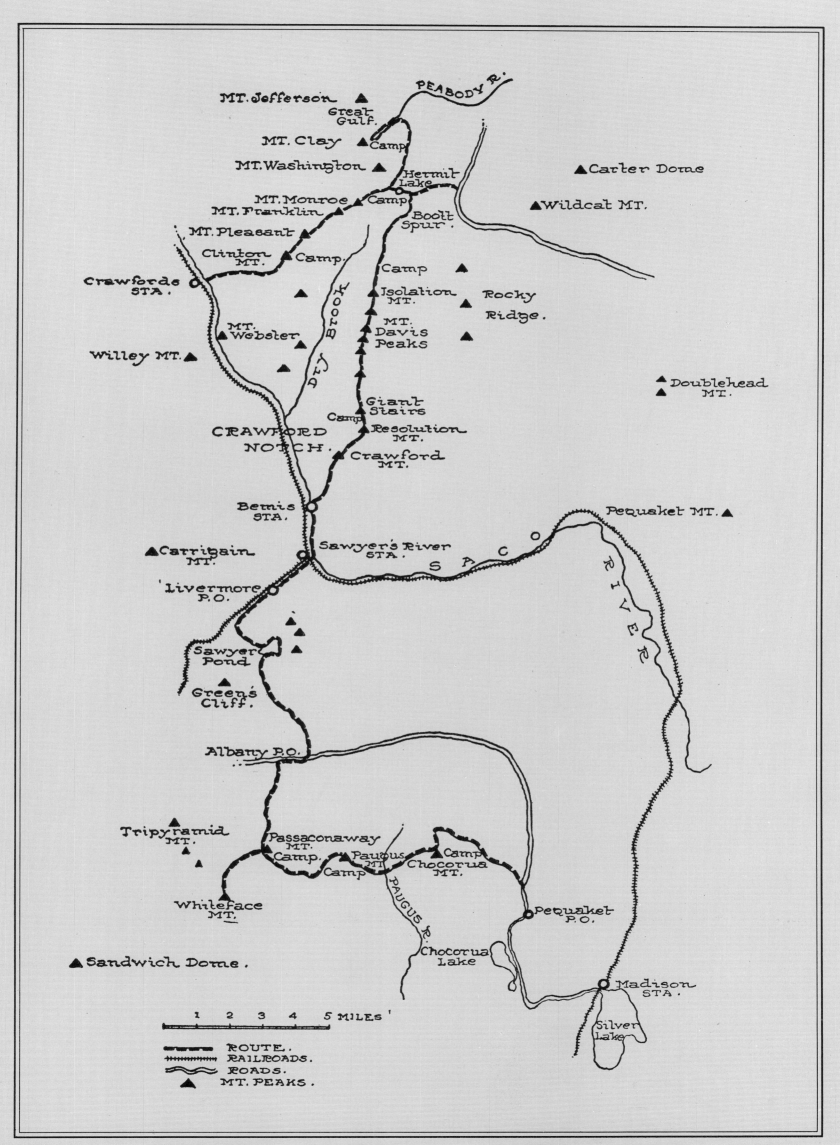

MT. Jefferson ▲

PEABODY R.

Great Gulf.

MT. Clay ▲ Camp

MT. Washington ▲

Hermit Lake

▲ Carter Dome

MT. Monroe ▲ Camp

MT. Franklin ▲

Boott Spur.

▲ Wildcat MT.

MT. Pleasant ▲

Clinton MT. ▲ Camp.

Camp

Crawfords STA. ○

▲ Isolation MT.

Rocky Ridge.

▲

MT. Webster ▲

MT. Davis Peaks ▲

▲

Willey MT. ▲

▲

▲ Doublehead MT.

▲

Giant Stairs

Camp

CRAWFORD NOTCH.

▲ Resolution MT.

▲ Crawford MT.

Bemis STA. ○

Pequaket MT. ▲

▲ Carrigain MT.

Sawyer's River STA.

SACO RIVER

Livermore P.O. ○

▲▲

Sawyer Pond ▲

Green's Cliff.

Albany P.O.

Tripyramid MT. ▲

Passaconaway MT. Camp.

▲ Paugus MT.

Camp Chocorua MT.

▲

Camp

PAUGUS R.

Whiteface MT.

Pequaket P.O. ○

▲ Sandwich Dome.

Chocorua Lake

Madison STA. ○

Silver Lake

1 2 3 4 5 MILES

ROUTE.

RAILROADS.

ROADS.

▲ MT. PEAKS.

From *Skyline Promenades*, by Brooks Atkinson, 1925